BC 4?

CHARITY
Is a Contact Sport

*Move from a Life of Success
to a Life of Significance*

Mitchell S. Morrison

WINEPRESS  PUBLISHING

© 2002 by Mitchell S. Morrison. All rights reserved.

Printed in the United States of America.

Packaged by WinePress Publishing, PO Box 428, Enumclaw, WA 98022. The views expressed or implied in this work do not necessarily reflect those of WinePress Publishing. The author is ultimately responsible for the design, content, and editorial accuracy of this work.

Unless otherwise noted, all scriptures are taken from the Holy Bible, New International Version, Copyright © 1973, 1978, 1984 by the International Bible Society. Used by permission of Zondervan Publishing House. The "NIV" and "New International Version" trademarks are registered in the United States Patent and Trademark Office by International Bible Society.

ISBN 1-57921-385-5
Library of Congress Catalog Card Number: 2001089472

ACKNOWLEDGMENTS

This book is dedicated to Susie Woy, my tireless assistant, one of the hardest working persons I know in any business, and to the family who blesses me with the reality that nothing is more important than family: my children Reed and Kaylen; my brother David, who financially backed our company, Charitable Alliance Group, and has been an extremely valuable guiding light; and lastly my wife Bonnie, who has seen and experienced the highs, the lows, the bold, the brave, the longing, the lost, and the found.

Mitchell Morrison, President, Charitable Alliance, presenting a check to Pastor John Wynn, Tabernacle of Praise Church, Sacramento, California.

CONTENTS

Mitchell Morrison, Candyce Bourgeois, and Juanita Wynn standing in front of new church purchase due to fund-raising efforts of Charitable Alliance Foundation for Tabernacle of Praise Church.

FOREWORD

Philanthropy is a combination of two words, *phileo* and *anthropos*. *Phileo* means the love for brother or sister. *Anthropos* describes mankind and all of humanity. A philanthropist is one who loves humanity and demonstrates that love through gifts.

Charitable Alliance Foundation's Mission Statement: The most powerful ingredient in life is love. Love motivates people to perform exceptional acts in the name of human compassion. The Charitable Alliance Foundation creates an esprit de corps throughout the world in serving charitable needs. All mankind is served when charity is preserved.

Increasingly we view a world overwhelmed with needs and lacking hope. Yet the process for fulfillment is neglected. Charitable Alliance Foundation takes great pleasure to facilitate, serve, and dedicate major resources to serving human need. Our mission needs include: medical facilities, medical response, children, biblical outreach, education, food distribution, preservation of natural resources, and housing.

Under supervision of Dr. Kenton Beshore and Dr. Ernest Vandeweghe, the Grants Outreach program and the Donor

Advised Outreach program can both serve numerous causes and charitable efforts. The hard-earned experience of the board members, the executive director and foundation employees create a connection between hoping miracles will happen and allowing miracles to occur.

Charitable Alliance Foundation
P.O. Box 53456
Irvine, CA 92619-3456
Phone: (877) GIVING3
Office: (714) 456-1794
Website: charitablealliances.org
Three dollars on each copy of this book sold will be donated to charity.

Mitchell Morrison and Marshall Faulk, National Football League MVP, teaming up to help Tabernacle of Praise Church.

INTRODUCTION

The major challenge and the reasons for writing this book come from just about everywhere the eyes can see, the ears can hear, and wherever the rest of our senses reveal dire human and environmental needs. The current global situation compels us to understand that "giving is living and living means giving." Families and individuals are discovering that making a difference and giving in meaningful ways are vital to mankind.

As I reflect on my twenty-one years of research into finance, wealth accumulation, wealth preservation and wealth transfer, I have realized that most charities have not done their homework. This inductive reasoning on my part is pretty much hands-on and time-tested.

There were two questions that compelled me to write this book. First, how did the well informed protect their assets, manage their tax liabilities and continue to pass wealth from generation to generation? Second, if most of the very wealthy have been using charitable strategies for

Mitchell Morrison and Minnesota Vikings Coach, Dennis Green, attending the Cris Carter, NFL Man-of-the-Year Award dinner, honoring the most outstanding man in the National Football League.

years, why don't the charities themselves actually understand these techniques and apply them with identified donors? If the charities are too busy with a vision itself and not the plan to complete the vision, they need to wake up to the possibilities.

Fortunately, I was able to work with several experts over the years who have educated me and inspired me to push forward in my quest. I wish to thank Dr. Bob Seaberg, president of CitiGroup Estate and Trust Services Division; Dr. Arthur Laffer; Herschel Gulley, national philanthropist; Kevin Hart, President, Sun America Securities; Dr. Steven Berry, Pastor First Congregational Church of Los Angeles; Dr. Ernest Vandeweghe, M.D., Patricia Riley, Esq.; David Sprowl, Esq.; David Morrison, CFO, Consolidated Freightways, Trustee Central States Teamsters Union and, also, my brother; Dr. Kenton F. Beshore and Lois Beshore, World Bible Society. Further inspiration is accredited to: Fred L. Morrison, Sophie Morrison, Rebecca Morrison and Susie Jones. Of course the real credit must be given to my wife Bonnie, my son Reed, and my daughter Kaylen. They provide the reasons for the passion. It is the benefit of the loved that inspires this book and my quest. Furthermore, using God as my guiding light and my faith, I push forward.

All of life I consider a gift from God, yet it gives me great pleasure to affirm and acknowledge those whom I love, respect, trust and confide in. If I can leave this world better off through my small contribution of knowledge and focused execution pertaining to strategic giving, then I become a more serious man.

I suppose someone becomes "serious" when you realize that there are things in life that seem to hit you in the face. The most dramatic revelations come to a person when you have actually seen the two opposite ends of the spectrum. The difference between going off the deep end and coming back is knowing just how deep and how high things can get. This education process requires pushing the envelope and not just thinking "outside the box" but *going* outside the box. This expression has been used often in the business world. I consider it a visual statement that probably achieves its purpose. As it pertains to charity, there really should be no existence of a box, no limits to what we dream and fulfill for humanity. In business we solve problems. In charity we solve problems. The only difference is that the success achieved has a different reward system. Charity never fires you for helping out or lending a hand. Charity seems to give something and receive nothing in return. Wealth, fame and power will fade away, yet one charitable act can never be taken away from your life's work, your legacy as viewed by God, your family, and your peers.

I will discuss (good or bad) new words and phrases that are creeping into the standard language of philanthropy, words like Advanced Stewardship, Planned Giving, Advanced Philanthropy, Creative Stewardship, "Give while you live" and "Just Give It!" (Did someone steal that from "Just Do It"?) This is the new language of charity. Hopefully you will learn from this book whether they have true meaning or false and selfish meaning.

I will try to stay away from the overuse of legalese terms such as: testor, intestate, grantor, pour-over will, NIMCRUT (which stands for Net Income with Make up Charitable Remainder Uni-Trust), and my favorite, STEALTH (which stands for Strategic Transfer of Estate Assets Legally Toward Heirs).

I also bring a warning to all the financial services companies and institutions: invite the charity to your party before the charity has a party of its own, and you're not invited. This means that these giant financial institutions have not been kind to charity. The evidence speaks for itself. The great financial minds at MBA schools such as Harvard University, Stanford University, and University of Pennsylvania Warton School of Business, have not taught the individual charities and their affinity groups advanced estate planning and charitable gifting techniques. In addition, the techniques that have been trickled down to smaller or local charities are actually the wrong techniques! They do not benefit charities in a meaningful way. The techniques still being discussed do, in fact, benefit the commissioned financial advisor, the CPA firm, the legal team and, of course, the donor. The point is: The donor and the charity must benefit first and foremost!

Make no mistake about it, I am an advocate for the financial advisor, the CPA, the attorney, but insist on working with the ones that are trained and informed. These professionals must understand the difference between financial capital, social capital, and greed.

This book is intended to show people how to be themselves when it comes to philanthropy: to do what is best and most comfortable for your family wealth and assets. With charity comes some "giving up," yet the strategies that can be implemented are not only positive in the sense of leveraging your gifts, these strategies also leverage and increase your family's wealth. Financial management has proven that you can have what you want over time. Charitable management will prove that others can have what they need over time. Charitable giving should be a marathon, not a sprint. It should not be conducted in a "knee-jerk" fashion. I suggest anyone interested in kicking up their philanthropy a notch or two must acquire professional advice and seek out these advanced gifting techniques.

Who wins by reading this book? Only those who practice what they read! These strategies and techniques are available. They are being used. I can say that I am proud of myself for having the patience to learn these techniques and apply them. They can and will make a difference, a huge difference, in all our lives . . . now and in the future.

There is something new in the foundation world. I call it "reverse wealth." No, that is not a politically correct term for people who are poor or "fiscally challenged." It is describing people who are giving a *reverse tithe*. Instead of giving away one-tenth of your income per year, it equates to giving away to a charitable cause ten times the amount you spend on yourself.

I first read about this in a magazine article featuring Sir John Templeton. Everyone in the financial world knows this man who started Templeton Funds, now Franklin Templeton Funds, one of the largest and most successful asset managers in the world today! Sir John Templeton is one of the few people in the world who have discovered how to achieve this incredible transition from success, to wealth, to a life of significance. Sir John was knighted in England for his many visionary philanthropic efforts on a global basis. Sir John Templeton has developed a superior investment mind and attitude towards the greater goal. This has enabled him to understand the NEW CHARITY.

The New Charity is not mystical or magical. The New Charity is simply one phrase, which can be repeated forwards or backwards: GIVING IS LIVING and LIVING IS GIVING. In the New Charity you can go forward and you can go back at the same time. A charitable act or event can move forward shaping the future and improving things. The same charitable act can go back in time and fix things that need to be fixed. I know this concept sounds too good to be true, but it is true. If you believe that there are really no boundaries to hold us back, that we can move forward with all of our dreams, then you will get something out of this book. My research helped and enabled me to understand the "New Charity." I hope the following chapters in this book will help you understand it as well. Giving is living; living is giving; what a concept!

Last but not least, this book will encourage you to STOP GIVING to charity. Instead this book is going to show how you can make a greater impact by investing in charity. The act of giving usually becomes a single event. Although giving can be repeated over and over again, it still is considered an event. When you invest in something, then it becomes a process with strategy, tactics and timing issues. This is what the "New Charity" is about, making the results greater because the whole activity has moved from a single event of giving to the ongoing process of reliability. The charitable causes do not have to change nor do individual charities need to reshape themselves. The INVESTMENT OF CHARITY will be the focus of this book. The impact that can and will be made on our lives is just beginning to take shape. I know I am looking forward to experiencing it. I hope you will look forward to the changes and the dramatic impact as well!

GET READY FOR A BIG CHANGE: IT IS COMING SOONER THAN YOU THINK!

"When you reach that fork in the road—take it!"
—Yogi Berra

I love this quote because there comes a time in everyone's life when situations will present themselves with a different perspective. I ask you to never be afraid of change, because others are going to be with you. Change will bring about clarity in your life, and your quest for a greater purpose will become achievable.

The amazing fact that we have just completed a millennium should serve as a wake-up call for the entire planet. The changes that the entire world has seen and experienced seem mind boggling, to say the least. Our world would always hope for the best but must also prepare for the worst. The best is hopefully yet to come, and it could be conversely stated that the worst might be yet to come! Who knows for certain? The goal must be the people's awareness of the challenges that exist today. Those same challenges will be the major factors in how our lifestyles will be played out. It is not just about the differences between the haves and the have-nots. The real story lies in how we all care about each other and in our view of the future.

Many changes did take place during this last millennium, far too many to count up, but I hope you are ready, folks, because "You ain't seen nothin' yet!" The next 100 years will make the last 100 years pale in comparison. A real wild ride should be expected! Yet this author predicts that many of these unforeseen challenges will come at us from the blind side. We will not see them coming. The best offense for this "wild ride" may just be a shift, which takes insight and foresight. Working harder will be replaced by working smarter. This is already here in our society. At no time in history have so many become wealthy in such short timeframes. Recently it was reported that the fastest-growing family category in America today happens to be the segment where household wealth has grown to over one million dollars per family.

The "New Charity" is also about the new everything: the new technology, the new generation, and the new way of learning and applying what we learn. But most of all the greatest impact will be the new social values we embrace and the specific actions we exercise in holding on to those social values or deciding to change those values. The reward system we have been accustomed to will be changing. The ability to "feel good" will not be based on what we own, because that will not be fulfilling. Instead the belief will grow that a time has come to wonder what the possibilities could be, based on how we use what we own and what we know. The vast resources of the Internet started the revolution. The human spirit and compassion that inherently exist as man's best and brightest virtues will keep the movement going. Humans and our passions must also balance out what the Internet is creating. The human race cannot afford to go overboard with the Internet without differentiating all the information available and selecting social values. It would be wonderful if the internet would showcase the following quote.

> "To laugh often and much;
> To win the respect of intelligent people
> And affection of children; to earn the
> Appreciation of honest critics and endure
> The betrayal of false friends:
> To appreciate beauty, to find the best in others;
> To leave the world a bit better, whether by a
> healthy child, a garden patch or a
> Redeemed social condition; to know even
> One life has breathed easier because you
> have lived. *This is to have succeeded.*"

—Ralph Waldo Emerson

❧ *Chapter One* ☙

THE TITANIC WAS FOR SPEED—
THE ARK WAS FOR NEED
Finding a Purpose

This book will not actually discuss the details and differences between the famous Ark, built by Noah and his family, and the infamous Titanic, built by the finest shipbuilders of the day. If you were asked today which of these two ships should be chosen for a boat ride, there would not be much of a decision to be made, based on our knowledge of past history. The people who sailed on the Titanic sensed no impending danger. Their goal was to reach the United States in record time. The Titanic made a lot of sense. It was a Titan of a ship and it was built for speed. In sharp contrast, the people who drifted on the Ark did so purely out of faith alone. It bears pointing out again: professionals, considered the finest ship builders of their day, built the Titanic; amateurs, who had never before built any vessel, built the ark.

These ships represent the ongoing struggle of life. Many of us look at life in contrasts. The struggle represents a question: do we take the fastest ship in order to achieve our individual goals of wealth, power, influence, pleasure, self-indulgence? Or would we choose to look around and see whom we can gather together with before we board any ship and set sail into life's dangerous waters? Is passion and compassion a priority in our lives? Do others really matter? The people who believed Noah and his story took a great risk and survived the ordeal. The people who chose the Titanic took very little risk and paid dearly for it. When it comes to searching for ways to help charity in a meaningful fashion, the comparison between the Ark and the Titanic is significant. Similar to life's endeavors are also the endeavors of philanthropy. The quick fix will not work with charity. This chapter discusses where to find the passion and purpose that suits you and your family. This chapter also discusses where you won't find passion and purpose.

This next section deals with what I call the ultimate quest for speed. Look out! The Titanic is back, and it has a new name: THE INTERNET.

GET LOGGED OFF!
GET REAL!
GET A LIFE!

9 MYTHS OF THE INTERNET

MYTH #1. "The Internet allows me to 'think outside the box!'"

I think nothing could be further from the truth. Many innovative people built the Internet, but now that it has been built, simply using it may not produce "thinking outside the box." Your computer is a box! If you are glued to it, you are likely to be captured inside this box and lose a tremendous amount of creativity. The Internet is already a huge collection of "junk" that hinders clarity and focus. To put it mildly, the distractions on the Internet web pages are overwhelming. The Internet is information overkill in a very disorganized setting. I believe Charles Dickens said it best, "I never could have done without the habits of punctuality, order and diligence . . . the determination to concentrate myself on one subject at a time."

This means that the Internet is better utilized as a tool and not as a way of life. The quest for focus and clarity of purpose will be difficult if the Internet becomes someone's only learning and thinking device. Neither is it a way to guide a life in the right social direction. It is believed by many that the Internet is our salvation, moving us headlong into the future. The Pentium world and the Internet/ virtual world may possibly be responsible for creation of a culture that creates extreme inwardness. This is creating a me-oriented society that could overlook the wisdom of charity and ignore compassion. There is a risk that people will become more attached to the computer they own (or which owns them) than to other humans.

MYTH # 2. "The Internet will allow me to meet more people if I use it as a communication device."

The optimum word is "meet." Did anybody see the motion picture *You've Got Mail* starring Tom Hanks and Meg Ryan? The fact is, the Internet diverts attention from face-to-face meetings and actually promotes artificial meetings. An actual meeting must be arranged at a later date.

The event of actually having physical contact with other human beings could possibly become less and less if we continue to use the Internet as organized voyeurism. There are not any statistics on this, but many of us would bet that people are certainly using the Internet as a screening mechanism and choosing not to meet people right away. This could be a good way to screen people, but it also would not give a person a chance to make a first impression. A first impression reveals quite a bit. For those of us who go with our "gut" feelings, the Internet is not the preferred screening mechanism.

MYTH # 3. "I can spend more time with my family if I use the Internet."

Is this a trick statement? The sheer time that individual family members are spending logged-on is approaching that of television watching. Most adults and children watch television about 16 hours per week. In some households Internet usage far exceeds television watching. With television, individuals can all watch the same program together as a family. The family, however, is not utilizing the Internet together; the individual members of the household are not logging on as a family. Everyone in the household is logging on for different reasons and at different times. If you do some quick math and assume that each household has one internet phone line and each person (Mom, Dad, Sis or Brother) chooses to get on line for two hours each day, then that is a full eight-hour timeframe where the family could not possibly all be together (assuming one of the four family members is on the separate Internet line).

MYTH # 4. "The Internet helps me do things more quickly, especially purchasing things."

The jury is still out on this one, folks! Home shopping network is about as fast as it gets. On that television program, a buyer can order in a matter of seconds and have delivery in three days. Most websites don't make that claim. Several times I have personally used the Yellow Pages along with my phone and a credit card, and I have found many items faster than by the Internet.

Technology is a good thing; broadband, microwave transmissions and other technological advances will make everything faster and faster. The question is, do we really need it that fast?

MYTH # 5. "The Internet saves me money."

The Internet does not save you money. You save yourself money. Smart consumers find that careful buying and comparison-shopping can be done at retail outlet malls, auctions, swap meets and flea markets. Furthermore, some studies show that bargains advertised on the Internet fall short of the above-named options.

MYTH # 6. "The Internet can get me a better job!"

The "Net" makes big promises but does not deliver on this one. The Gallup Organization report shows a decline by employers to use the Internet as a recruiting source. Many employers still prefer fax and mail to e-mail in receiving résumés for job applications.

I must admit if someone has no idea what type of career to choose or pursue then perhaps the "Net" may provide ideas and resources. Searching for a better job takes focus, networking, and interviewing real people who already work for one of the companies you wish to pursue.

MYTH # 7. "The Internet is the future of the New Economy."

A funny thing happened on the way to the Dot-Com Company:

Dot-com no sales!
Dot-com no capital!
Dot-com no service!
Dot-com no product!

It is unfortunate that many investors will lose billions on Internet stocks. Advancement of the Internet does not really equal advancement of profits. The Internet has created many millionaires and e-commerce is still the hottest and fastest way to make millions. Net incubators and venture capital firms will still search for the next "Yahoo." I encourage the average person who can't afford taking risks with their hard earned dollars to be very careful before they jump back into Internet stocks.

MYTH # 8. "The Internet makes my life simpler!"

This statement has turned into the ultimate catch-22. The problem with the Internet is not where do I find it, but how do I organize it? Prioritize it? How will it interface with keeping my life on track? The Internet is a hindrance to the highest and best use of your time. This author believes that valuable time with loved ones and the balance between work and play may best be achieved with a simple time management course and a daily calendar.

Palm pilots and hand-held organizers are also great tools. It is not necessary to spend endless hours on the Net, or on your computer, for that matter, to get organized and stay organized.

MYTH # 9. "The Internet can help me find my purpose."

Finding a true purpose includes many things. Changes may help you reconsider your life. The struggle of life may help you find a purpose. Common sense and ethical values may help you find a purpose. It is extremely doubtful that life's meaning can be found on the Internet. If somebody is searching for purpose on the Net, I recommend they cease. Furthermore, 78% of adolescent students have admitted visiting *objectionable* websites. Objectionable websites are sites promoting hate groups, pornography, violence, and music banned by the F.C.C. I recommend that finding purpose will be achieved when we experience the following: love, sharing, compassion and granting peace to each other. These can only be experienced face to face. Purpose, like charity, is also a contact sport.

The last but not least problem with the Internet is that the Internet does not give you feedback and does not provide a real support system for your purpose. Don't take my word for it. Log on and try your luck! Good luck!

Winning the Lottery Is Another "Titanic."
Be Careful What You Wish For!

50% of all Lotto winners file bankruptcy within 2 years (source: Dunn & Bradstreet). The average American has a total net worth, after debts and liabilities, of $56,000 (source: Dunn & Bradstreet). Why is this the case? This author believes it is due to lack of purpose for individuals and families. It is your life; solutions become clear when you focus on the refinement of your purpose. Most people will focus on the system that rewards skill and effort rather than reputation. Our environment is affecting our life decisions because it is what we do and where we exist day after day. It is through our reputation that we can all receive our strength and the ability to be somebody unique. Finding who you are based on reputation will also help you find that sense of purpose.

If you are over 25 years of age, believe it or not . . . you have a reputation! Now is the time to work with that reputation and declare, perhaps for the first time, that you wish to focus on making a difference. When people adopt a lifestyle that is based on a purpose that includes helping others, then their lives become dramatically enriched. A person's reputation could be his greatest asset. At some point, most of us stop trying to just make a living and start focusing on how to make a life. When you have a daily philosophy of being a giver, and you develop the habit of helping others with no immediate thought of personal reward, you begin to realize your sense of purpose.

What does my reputation mean to others?

Your reputation may be positive, but is it significant? When you focus on your reputation, do you ask: What is my life's work all about? What am I doing right now with my life? What will be my legacy? How will my friends and family be affected by my demise?

THE CHALLENGE

Let others lead small lives . . . but not you.
Let others argue over small things . . . but not you.
Let others cry over small hurts . . . but not you.
Let others leave their future in someone else's hands . . . but not you.
—Jim Rohr

I suggest that everyone who wishes to begin the journey also begin by writing a charitable business plan. All business plans have a "mission statement." A mission statement will define the purpose and define the goal. The next steps are to develop a plan of action or a set of action steps. This means finding which changes need to take place in your life to make a positive difference every day. The next step is to figure out what resources you bring to the party and who you can recruit to join your quest.

The following are examples of mission statements:

"To inspire and empower families to live at their highest vision, encouraging love, tolerance and joy."

"To assist, financially and with outside resources, battered families and the poor."

"To inspire my associates, co-workers and clients with wisdom and solutions that will make a difference in the lives of the less fortunate."

The mission statement should be short and sweet, and also realistic. If you are familiar with the *Chicken Soup for the Soul* series, you know they have a mission statement. It is: "To change the world, one story at a time."

The last step in this process is to make sure you do not get stuck on a horizontal path. People at this level may have no interest in learning more or in significantly improving themselves, even though it will improve their lifestyle. Life will again become routine if all the focus rests with security and survival. As long as they can keep their jobs, watch TV, pay the bills, then they keep disaster at bay. People are not winners if preserving the status quo is their focus. People will tend to blame situations for lack of success but won't plan to change themselves. Because everything in life is a choice, many of us will choose to stay right where we are. Beginning a transition requires a vertical movement, not a horizontal movement. Working harder and longer each day will only bring you more of what you already have. Increasing your level of performance is a good thing in beating the competition, but it may not actually affect someone's life in a positive manner. Increasing your work output may just maintain your time on the treadmill of working faster and harder.

In today's world, finding a purpose may be our only choice of true self worth. The vast changes in technology and the evolvement of the Internet are beginning to neutralize individual talents. Seeking the advice of experts in a specialized field is no longer a difficult task. What can't you get from the Internet today? In addition, the way we think is changing. The pre-Internet age was based on, "I'll stay unless you give me a reason to go." The Internet age says, "I'll go unless you give me a reason to stay!" This brings a whole new spin to doing business in today's highly competitive world. If everyone has access to the same information, and we can all share the same resources, then how do we differentiate ourselves? This answer will not come from the Internet. The answer will come from developing unusual clarity with the ability to create exciting pictures of the future.

The promise of success will materialize if you make the effort to develop the habit of unusual clarity; the payoff for you or your business down the road will be tremendous. Clarity will eventually lead to the higher concept of brilliance. To find your brilliance, ask yourself a few questions: What do you do effortlessly, without study or preparation?

What else can you do that others find difficult? These same people gasp at your ability and cannot come close to it. We are all blessed with God-given talents. A big part of your life so far has been discovering what these are and applying them to your best ability. This discovery process can take years for many people, and some never actually find it. Consequently, those lives are less fulfilled. These people tend to struggle because they spend valuable time in jobs or businesses not suited to their strengths. Finding your purpose will increase your focus, increasing focus will produce clarity, which brings about brilliance. Last but not least, brilliance will determine the size of your opportunities in life.

The Devil is in the details—up to 90 percent of our normal behavior is based on habits.

Many of our daily activities are simply routines. From time to time you may get up in the morning and, until you go to bed in the evening, there are hundreds of activities you do the same way. This will include the way you get ready for the day, the way you eat breakfast, read the news, attend meetings, schedule your appointments, work on your computer, and so on. As creatures of habit we can become very predictable creatures. However, with too much routine, complacency sets in and then boredom.

> If you keep on doing what you've always done,
> You'll keep on getting what you've always got!

All good people will choose to do good deeds over time. The question of when these good deeds will become an individual quest and a priority is different for each of us. The timing towards a desire in this area may be based on where someone is with his or her life. Timing can be everything, in many cases. The people who will best benefit from this book are the ones who believe that "making a difference" is more important and significant than making money alone or getting on the fastest ship (like the Titanic). To Noah, as told in the Bible, caring for others was not an option! On the other hand taking the fastest ship, the Titanic, was an option that everyone could afford to miss.

Chapter Two

A FUNNY THING HAPPENED ON THE WAY TO THE CHARITY!

Meaningless! Meaningless! says the teacher. Utterly meaningless. Everything is meaningless. What does a man gain from all his labor at which he toils under the sun? Generations come and generations go, but the earth remains forever. The sun rises and the sun sets and hurries back to where it rises. What has been will be again. What has been done will be done again. There is nothing new under the sun. Is there anything of which one can say, "Look! This is something new"? It was here already, long ago, it was here before our time. (Ecclesiastes 1:2–10)

I wonder when I read this scripture, *Is this some secret code that I do not understand?* The teaching of the teacher seems to be representing the "Happiness Prevention Team." What is the point after all that? It's not enough to know that with all the suffering, pain, starvation and hate in the world that the teacher in the Bible says, "All things are wearisome, more than one can say." As I read these passages over and over, my mind races toward our final destiny, and then I ask, "What does it matter and what difference can I make?" Many people ask, "How can I help put a dent in the world's problems? How can I make a difference? If I make a difference, who will know? Who will care?" The specific question by many folks with good hearts becomes, "How I can help anyone, much less the whole world?"

The answer to that question, "How can I help make a difference?" will be found by reading the above scripture over and over again. Suddenly you will have the answer appear before you. The answer is: You just help! The announcement, the fanfare, the game plan, is not important. What is important is that you begin. Goodness consists in knowing the good, desiring the good and doing the good. In the introduction of this book is the statement, "Giving is Living." What this means today is quite significant in the process of the New Charity. If we take the attitude that serving and giving is a regular part of our lives and of our growth as a human race, then things become different.

Instead of looking at the world with the view of the Old Charity, we must realize the power and effectiveness of the New Charity. The difference between the Old Charity and the New Charity is that the Old Charity never said giving is living. In fact the Old Charity made many of us fearful of giving because there might not be enough food, clothing, shelter or warmth to go around for everybody. The stories of sacrifice, fasting, protest and even crusades were the ways of the world and are still based on the fact that the strong will rule the weak and the weak will suffer. The more things change, the more they stay the same. Ever heard that one before? I would like to change that phrase to: the more we change, the more things will get better.

The Old Charity is unforgiving in many ways. The Old Charity existed with three components: the Cause, the Struggle, and the Victory. Most human beings deemed the Old Charity to be necessary wherever the pragmatic line was drawn between the Haves and the Have-Nots. Our views have been defined, and this has been the view of our society. Humans additionally have a much easier time looking back rather than forward. This weakness has haunted mankind and in itself may be the single biggest reason why charity has been slow to move forward and bring about significant consistent results. Pragmatic solutions to produce results can only become consistent if a visionary's strong will is followed. At the same time, this visionary has to come up with an ability to convince others to accept change. The visionary must be a leader and a salesperson who is animated in a way that creates a sense of urgency. In other words, the Old Charity would require a strong leader who could convince others that their cause was indeed very worthy.

In contrast, the New Charity is about inspiring excellence in all people attached to the process. A director of a New Charity might say something like, "I don't care who came up with the idea! Let's all break into teams so we can expand the idea and network into the system." The New Charity is about making sure the resources are in place to make tremendous improvement in meeting human needs on a global basis. Technology will allow these changes to occur because technology for once will be able to actually execute and not just theorize these changes. But what must really happen is that we must change. I mean, each person must change the way he or she thinks. The motivating factors of selfishness, power, greed, fear and resentment must be abandoned. The question "Why should I help?" should no longer be a question at all! Stewardship is not an option, either! If you read the Bible you will note that there is a defender of the poor, and this defender is very strong indeed. That defender is God himself. Proverbs states; "Do not exploit the poor because they are poor, for the Lord will take up their case and plunder those who plunder them."

I worked for a marvelous salesman. His name was Marty Barrett. He said to me, "It's impossible to close a sale if you forgot to open." Charity is about the heart and the needs of others. Ego is left at the door. A desire to begin the process by learning about needs, goals and solutions is much better than an attitude of, "My way worked in business, and it will work with charity." If we agree "Giving Is Living," then we must also see that work is giving, also. This means that the workplace is also a key element of bringing about change and helping others. With most of us consumed in work for the longest stretch of our lives, we now need a focus of channeled energy towards philanthropy during the workday. Focusing on the difference between generating profits and generating deeds needs to happen at the precise same time. In Chapter Ten, Alliance Charities, you will also see the positive effects of alliance businesses. These are businesses that are making a difference, and they are making this difference "on company time."

In many cases, business disciplines will work just fine in charity. However, people need to understand that you can't forget to open a sale first. The only way you can help charity is to begin as a servant, not as a boss. Be humble in your resolve and nurture your own learning curve. Don't question your degree of passion or your worthiness. How you communicate your goodness will not help other people. How you communicate the worthiness of the needs and fulfillment of the needs will help other people. Recently a church worker stated to me, "I enjoy life when I *do* God, not when I talk God." I've seen numerous volunteers come into a charitable activity and start giving orders to fulfill what they want and believe is the best tactic. However, this is called "closing before you begin to open." You must establish your passion, your heart, and your loyalty *before* you can run a charity like a boss.

It is a fact that our religious services are about the understanding of historical events with divine characters: Jesus Christ, Mohammed, Buddha, Joseph Smith, Woody Allen (just kidding about Woody!). All of their teachings, whether Gospel, Holy Scriptures, Talmud, Koran, Book of Mormon, or other, purport to be a guide to living your life according to absolute spiritual purpose. Why is there no mention of the Internet, cell phones, politically correct language, women in the workplace, and all the other current "answers" for life? People are struggling with acceptance and the mystery of wondering, "How should I live my life?" Being politically correct is old news. Now is the time to be charitably correct.

Philanthropy will help. It is interesting to note that there is no bad giving or sacrificing to helping others. Think about it. If you get confused about how to live your life, then remember there is no bad giving; by giving your time, services or money to help others, you will be happier, healthier and more productive.

Let's look at world needs. There are 6 billion people in the world today, and 4 billion live on less than $1,500 (U.S.) per year. That's approximately $3.75 per day. If that statistic bothers you . . . it gets worse! The average Haitian makes $19,500 in a lifetime. Michael Eisner, CEO, Walt Disney Company, makes $19,500 a *minute*. In 1999, in the United

States, the poverty level was $17,560 for a family of four (Source: New York Times, 1999). Therefore, Michael Eisner makes $1,940 more than this family the first minute he gets on the job. If you're a math geek, you know that Mr. Eisner made over the annual poverty level in 54 seconds.

One out of every four children in America still goes to bed hungry. (Source: Feed the Children). How many people do you personally know in your neighborhood who need or want for food? The truth can be so stark when we see it up close, touch it, or experience it firsthand. There is always a difference when things happen or are exposed before our eyes. The laundry list of good causes actually grows every day. People are beginning to embrace more causes.

Last year charitable donations were $175 billion in the United States. However, there is significant bad news. Charitable giving, as it pertains to a percentage of income, has remained constant for the last thirty years. That number is still only 2% of income. And . . . to make matters worse, the number of family and community foundations has grown to over one million non-profits. More may actually turn out to be less. Competition for government and private money is fierce. The larger organizations have enormous advantages over the local ones. Less than 4% of the 501(c)(3) organizations have assets greater than $10 million, yet they receive half of public support. Forty percent (40%) have assets less than $100,000 and receive less than 3% of the financial support offered.

If you do the math and divide the number of non-profits into the number of charities, then you'll come up with an equal number of $175,000 going to each charitable foundation. This may seem to be a large proportion if it was an individual family foundation, but this number would be very small if we were talking about a school, a hospital or a church. Even though the amount of money going into non-profits has grown, the amount going to each non-profit is less. Charity is picking up in awareness, but inefficiency is starting to rear its ugly head, and more cases of financial mismanagement and charitable abuses are in the papers every day.

In discussing where the money should go, the emerging millionaires have a very strong say, as well as their own individual desires for directing gifts. These new millionaires have also made money quickly but wish to give away their money very slowly. For example, the twenty-two billion-dollar Bill and Melinda Gates Foundation has given away less than 10% of this amount to actual charitable causes as of year-end 1999. Do not construe this as being stingy. It is wise to know the efficiency of one's giving. For Bill, it was easier making the money than giving it away!

Many of these people are confused about where to give their money, and are probably not in agreement that there is "no bad giving." The new outlook of social capital seems to be viewed as a research project by many new millionaires. They are determined to investigate causes, charities and needs, down to specific focus. Yet the wisdom taught by the Bible tells us in Proverbs 3:9–10, "Honor the Lord with your wealth, with the firstfruits of all your crops: then your barns will be filled to overflowing and your vats will brim over with new wine."

It's interesting that by giving we will be getting back more than we gave. Is this fantasy? Is this a possibility? Wouldn't it take magic to have this transformation take place?

Actually, it will take place and it will be a reality. Giving requires two things:
(1) Give with a glad heart; (2) Give with an educated mind.

Giving with an educated mind will give you a glad heart. Giving is about many things: information, education, awareness, experiences, life situations and a calling to serve. The divinity doesn't matter although motive always becomes an important issue. This book will take on the task of education and ways to use that education toward your own situation or for the situation of other donors whom you may know.

You will want to understand and control the knee-jerk emotions that move you in response to the pain, suffering and despair of others. You can kill yourself trying to save the world. It is also important to remember that in life it is the marathoner and not the sprinter that will win this race. The true hope lies in making progress. Progress must exist in the formula. People are frustrated, discouraged and exhausted when there is no progress.

Remember the definition of insanity: doing the same thing over and over, while expecting different results. Our outlook and our resolve will change along with strategies and tactics. If the well-run and well-intentioned charities can attract the wealthy donor, then this is great. However, don't count on that happening. The "new philanthropists" who have made their money quickly are giving their money away slowly. Furthermore, these "dot.com" millionaires and billionaires feel that the money they give away is still their money—still their money in the sense that the researching of charitable causes is more diligent by this group. Diligence in this area is okay, yet I learned two lessons that are time-tested in the area of giving. I'll call these Lesson #1 and Lesson #2.

Remember the sun is 330,000 times larger than the earth. Researchers who discovered this were, hopefully, looking for a bigger picture. The size of the sun has meaning, yet the importance of these facts could really be dramatic if it were discovered that the sun was getting larger each day. Well, in light of that (pardon the pun), let me give you the lessons as they pertain to charity:

**Lesson #1:   Charity is about others, not about you;
                  Charity is bigger than you!**

Charity is the next level, or a higher calling than what most of us consider our life's work. In all fairness to those who have concentrated on the precursors to a charitable life, we should debate these priorities first:

Family, God, Country, Community.
God, Family, Country, Community.
Country, Family, God, Community.
God, Country, Family, Community.

Any way you shake it out, community has always been last in the sequence. Have you ever heard a world leader or politician state that his priority is community before God, family, and country? Yet, if you still are not convinced that community is dead last, consider this: "Love thy neighbor as thyself." This was left as a clue that ignoring this Biblical mandate proves to be the beginning of all mass strife and suffering.

By putting community last, we have created a world with a huge gap. The Internet has demonstrated a world can be transformed almost overnight to move in the same direction. It took hundreds, perhaps thousands, of years for the majority of the world to hear about Jesus Christ. Today, a world leader, or better yet a rock star like Michael Jackson, would be recognized in a matter of minutes using the Internet.

If we summarize that technology is, in fact, bringing us together, then what does the word together mean? If it means our exposure to one another over video lines, e-mail, streaming media, and so on is causing community to occur, that is one idea we can embrace. But, if it means what many suspect, which is that all this technology is just an easy access to voyeurism and increasing our pre-judgments of others, then where have we come? At this point, who can really say? There are some very disturbing facts that should cause alarm with technology. Since the introductions of the Internet:

1. No creed, doctrine or religion has been formed or been successful in promoting goodwill and deterring violence.
2. More children ran away or are missing than ever before in the United States.
3. Crime is down (according to the Justice Department), but child abuse is up.
4. Teen drinking and smoking is up in the United States, and incidence of drunk driving among teens is up.
5. Most psychiatrists and psychologists agree that thoughts of suicide among teens have increased.

Do these things mean that technology is causing rise to these problems? No! Not really. But, it also indicates that better exposure to people through the electronic medium is not making the difference hoped for. What should we expect? The expectation of results may not lie in the fact that we have the technology or the access to view and communicate. Communication is not enough to promote community or caring for one another. Our attitudes must be affected in some way to wish involvement on our part and the part of others. The answer does not lie in creating the technology or increasing the technology. The answer lies in taking this technology with a game plan in mind.

Lesson #2: All charities are a black hole.

This means . . . everyone has his or her hand out. They sing for their supper, and they will be your best friends until the donations cease. So what does this mean?

It is called establishing a pipeline for charitable budgets. "You can lead a horse to water, but a pencil must be lead." I mean, a charity must be led toward goal getting, efficient planning and the ability to pass the torch even though the flame may flicker. The flame flickers when the dedicated, driven volunteers cease to volunteer or the executive director who no longer continues the work of the charity for some reason. This can occur because of death, sickness, change-of-heart, lack of spirit, or lack of resources, to name a few. The charity itself must have a good reason to continue and be supported. Hope is not enough, charities must have a sense of security and avoid false hope. False hope is worse for charities than no hope. Charities (at least the smaller ones) can be very dependent on one single gift or source of funds. When that source of funds is promised and not delivered, the end result is devastation. All of us who make promises to charities must be aware of this. The following is an example of innocent false hope actually caused by a national television broadcast.

The East Harlem School in New York City was recently featured as a charitable cause on the television show, *Who Wants to Be a Millionaire?* David Ducovny (actor featured on *The X-Files*) was on the show and had the opportunity to hit the one million dollars. He was on the second to the last question . . . the $500,000 question . . . and he gave the wrong answer. Well, as a result, the dollar amount fell back to $32,000. That number is $968,000 shy of one million. Why couldn't ABC give the benefit of the doubt and just give the million, or at least grant the $500,000? The Nielsen Ratings alone would have more than justified the amount, in my estimation. The advertisers probably would have been pleased either way. Talk about a letdown for this well-intentioned cause! Believe me, that extra $968,000 would have been very beneficial for the school.

The point is, charity should not be a gamble, and the fund-raising for charities can follow a process and needs to have a pipeline of funding. The charity itself must appoint someone who is informed and properly advised. This person must have some resources at their disposal and the perseverance to keep going. Remember what Woody Allen once said: "Ninety percent of all success is just showing up." I agree. Yet focus and goal setting need to be monitored. Your favorite charity may remain a "black hole" of always needing dollars, but there lies the challenge of the charities which will thrive and ones who will not.

The changes that are taking place in our private sector are beginning to have substantial impact on the philanthropic sector as we speak. The non-profits must also redefine themselves as business has done over the past 20 years. People want information and responses faster, with accuracy and sense of purpose. This sense of purpose must have unique qualities that can grab attention in today's fast-paced world. People will continue to lack patience and expect results under more demanding time frames. To use a quote from a very good Beatle song, "You've got to admit it's getting better—It's getting better all the time." That's what people expect today: getting better all the time.

❧ Chapter Three ☙

ATHLETES AND ENTERTAINERS IN THE CHARITABLE PROCESS?
If Charity Is a Contact Sport, You Must Make Contact

I f you are forty years old or more, you may have heard the expression, "He can't walk and chew a piece of gum at the same time." Well, sad to say, most athletes, actors, singers, and other famous entertainers can't give to charities and have their lifestyle at the same time, either! Now, I am not talking about these folks committing their time. (We will get into that later.) I am talking about pledging their own money. The actual amount that this group gives annually is quite low. Most people would expect the numbers to be very high in this area of giving. I will name a few individuals who have given large amounts to charities such as: Cris Carter wide receiver Minnesota Vikings, Charles Barkley formerly with the Phoenix Suns basketball team, and Paul Newman the famous actor. Athletes and entertainers, with more exceptions than named in this book, are for the most part small givers. Their giving as a percentage of income is less than the national average of 1.8% annually, and as a percentage of their overall wealth it is also quite low.

I would give a warning to these folks, that dressing up in a tuxedo and attending a charitable event several times a year does not constitute doing a big part for any charity! If you can handle the truth, most of these charitable events give complimentary tickets to big-name celebrities at these upscale bashes. This means they got in free where regular folks paid to attend and contribute. In addition, athletes and entertainers may have demanding schedules, but they are not tied down to an all-day-every-day situation like most Americans. I would conclude that if the celebrity has time to go to charity balls then he should also have time to volunteer on the front lines and figure ways to raise funds for the charity he presumably supports.

This author has chosen to not single out specific individuals or even groups. However, a famous athlete who will go unnamed made eleven million dollars last year and only gave $20,000 to charitable causes. That equates to less than one-quarter of one cent on the dollar. To make matters worse, many athletes and entertainers are setting up their own private foundations, which they believe helps fulfill their charitable passions. This is like having an accountant or lawyer become the head coach of a professional sports team. Coaching takes knowing the specialized techniques, the rules, the strategies and the changes occurring all the time. Running a private foundation can be just as complicated. Just ask Sammy Sosa, Tony Glynn and a host of others who have met with the federal government and heard the famous phrase, "My name is_____; I'm with the IRS and I'm here to help!" Another example would be that starting and running a private foundation is like going into the restaurant business. Restaurants have the highest failure rate of all categories of profit businesses in the United States. The restaurant business takes hands-on involvement and knowledge.

Most of us are shocked at the tremendous "bad publicity" athletes and entertainers are receiving all the time. It goes without saying that they are targets for media attention. However, are they targeted? Or are these famous people somewhat arrogant and disregard laws more than the average American citizen? If this is the case, then all celebrities should be jumping at the good will and good publicity that charitable activities will bring into their lives. The mistake they have been making is the lack of preparation and of consultative advice. The sports agent who negotiated their contracts is not the best skilled in the area of philanthropy. The sports agent's job is to make money for his client, not to research and find ways to give it out! This concept actually goes against the function of the professional sports agent.

The larger sports management agencies claim to serve their clients in this area. However, the case-by-case numbers of private foundations being cancelled by frustrated athletes is on the rise. It may be because a private foundation takes a high degree of maintenance, while sports agencies do not derive fees from a successful foundation. There is no incentive for the agent to learn this area well because he or she won't make any money from it. What should be instigated is pretty simple. The athlete or celebrity needs to find people who specialize in this area. Of course, this is somewhat difficult because there is not a lot of money made by a firm who specializes in giving out charitable advice and direction. Most of these firms have to derive their livelihood either from legal set-up fees or from specializing in investment strategies geared toward tax savings and charitable planning. If this charitable quest is truly a desire of all celebrities or athletes, then much more time must be dedicated to the educational process of the celebrity/athlete.

The need for increasing involvement of sports and entertainment personalities in philanthropy is very crucial at this point in time. At no other point in our history has the sports and entertainment industry been under such heavy attack. Sports can be considered competitive, aggressive, sometimes violent, to win at all costs because "winning isn't everything, it is the only thing," as Vince Lombardi said. Entertainment can also be considered violent, aggressive, competitive, with a win-at-all-costs attitude thanks to greed. The entertainment merger between sports and other entertainment is real as well as imagined. Keeping these fields apart will not happen in the future. The public perception is that violence is up in the sports world and also in television and movies. The other public perception is that these people, entertainers and athletes, are paid too much money. I personally believe that is more reality than perception! Last but not least, the sought-after high-profile celebrity likes his career and dedicates so much time to it that he neglects core values such as family and concern about living a significant life as opposed to just a highly successful career. There is nothing wrong with devotion to success; however, balancing success with "making a difference" is going to replace the emptiness left when you forsake all other achievements to accomplish success only.

If there were an area where celebrities and athletes could make a tremendous impact immediately for a charitable cause, it would be in the area of fundraising. The concept is simple, and anyone can see it right away. Fundraising is like a movement. It takes networking, teamwork, personality and communication, but most of all there must be a leader. Celebrities and athletes are leaders whether they like it or not. People want to be near them, people want to follow them, and people want to look up to them. This is great news. If the famous personality wants to raise money, he or she can do it better than anyone on this planet can. It is imperative that the cause be genuine, above reproach, have sound economics and at some point demonstrate positive results.

My Personal Situation

The best example I can give about making contact is a real live situation that happened in my own life. My father was an athlete and a celebrity. He played seven years in the National Football League as running back. He played four years with the Chicago Bears and three years with the World Champion Cleveland Browns. He made the Pro Bowl game three years in a row. In college he was a running back at Ohio State University, with the Big Ten champs, and was named the most valuable player in the Rose Bowl. He also starred in the college all-star game and was part of the defeat of the World Champion Philadelphia Eagles in 1950. After he retired from the NFL, he became a professional sportscaster with CBS Television. He had an announcer/color commentator position with CBS and actually preceded Frank Gifford.

I look back at my successful dad and my amazing mother, and I really remember only one thing: I remember how Dad and Mother demonstrated the way to appreciate others—not by merely telling us to appreciate others, but also by involving us directly in the process at an early age.

My father was an avid golfer. At one time he belonged to three different country clubs and frequented them all. My mother also was an incredible golfer, but not as obsessed as dads tend to get! On Sundays, before church and before golf, my dad would take me, and sometimes my younger brother, to the worst part of town, the section of

Columbus, Ohio, where white folks stuck out like a sore thumb when they visited the neighborhood. It was known back then as "where the coloreds live." My dad would always tell me never to call a black man or woman by insulting names. He said that everyone we were going to visit worked very hard at their jobs but didn't make much money. I learned the word "poor" could be more devastating than just lack of liquid assets. Poor can also mean inadequate housing, poor health, bad habits, smoking, drinking and drugs

The families we visited had two working spouses. The men mainly worked either at the Columbus Dispatch or at the country clubs as shoeshine men. They were always friendly and seemed to be closer to each other than folks in the neighborhoods I experienced growing up. This spirit always amazed me because, as a white person growing up, I always heard how many problems black people had and how many ordeals they had to suffer. This led me to believe that to be black was to be unhappy or at least to have been born with bad luck. Yet it seems to me that African Americans are nicer to each other than whites are. I am not referring to any statistics about family violence or neighborhood violence. I guess I am talking about passion toward each other. Compassion may be lacking in the tragedy of: gang shoot-outs, drive-bys and drug dealing. Yet the violence seems to be more spontaneous than directed, a survival mode of our youths in the stark, scary reality of feeling neglected by an otherwise prosperous society.

The shelter, food, clothing, education, family and surroundings that I experienced growing up in the Upper Arlington section of Columbus were far different from those in the lower north side of Columbus, Ohio, the black section. It was great to see the faces when we dropped off clothes, shoes, and food, although I never felt good when we dropped off items. I just felt sad and guilty that I had more material possessions. Kids are kids and they are incredibly impressionable. Yet I do not believe I misjudged the overall situation.

The poverty was stark and I wondered what they thought about being poor and seemingly unhappy. What really mattered to me at the time was that we were generous and we were reaching out, and that my father was caring enough to really make a difference, to make contact and not ignore or hide from the realities of life. I saw a great deal of wisdom in my father as well as empathy, the kind of empathy that seemed to work out because he had a plan and decided to carry out that plan. My father knew who he was when he was with the less fortunate, but more importantly, he knew what to do. It is immeasurably more important to know what it takes to help people than it is to worry about how to act around people. My father would always lead with the empathy that is rare in a lot of us. I see that as a gift, to have that kind of empathy. It can certainly lead to inspiration and hope.

WHAT CHANGES ARE TAKING PLACE TO CONNECT US?

Macro-level demographic trends are opening the doors and changing who the players are in the philanthropic game. Their backgrounds are changing, where they live is changing, and the end result is a tremendous diversity that was not the case just a few decades ago. People from different walks of life are now becoming the norm in the area of philanthropy.

The typical foundation of years past held to a tightly shielded institution accountable mostly to itself. It is ironic that an organization dedicated to doing good works may have been in fact an elitist institution. A typical charity would be dominated by board members who did not even represent the demographic regions the charity was designed to serve. It is no secret that several decades ago a philanthropist meant someone who could afford to help others simply because he had the means to support this activity without incurring their own financial hardships. Today's volunteer and paid foundation employees are people of different colors, different creeds, and come from mainstream society. The mainstream is changing rapidly. The demographics of change will open doors to people of lesser means than traditional philanthropists. The center of philanthropy has changed over the last few years. In 1998 California replaced New York as the home to the greatest number of new charities becoming active in philanthropy.

What Are the Circumstances That Will Keep People from Continuing Contact— Why Do Volunteers Burn Out?

If you can relate to the statement, "I wouldn't take this job for all the money in the world," you know what the definition of exhaustion and emotional burnout is. This statement addresses an area that does not receive a lot of attention. Of course, if you have been a volunteer (which means you are not being paid for services rendered), you know what I am referring to. The volunteer is a vital and extremely valuable part of just about every charitable institution. Yet, however vital, the volunteer is frequently a person who is taken for granted. The great leaders in this country have come from all walks of life, including charity. However, something is different. Something seems to be not right. Passion can be so strong in a charitable endeavor, yet the accomplishments are not as exact as they are in business, wars, protests and politics. Maybe the non-profit world doesn't expect as much. Or perhaps when the charities succeed, or exceed their goals, it is not enough. Not enough in the sense that, after goals are reached, there still may be so many things left undone that need to be accomplished as well.

This could lead to a sense of futility! A lot of people don't know what they are getting into when they volunteer. The work involved can be an awesome task. It seems overwhelming when a volunteer first realizes the sheer numbers of needy persons. Another reality becomes very vivid when you realize that the people you are helping are really just like you! This can motivate yet drive a volunteer to the brink of exhaustion and obsession with the cause. The word passion becomes transformed to an activity that may *consume* a volunteer almost immediately, from the time they involve themselves with the charity. The human bonds that are formed when people help each other are incredible. There also is reliable proof that, when you help someone while expecting nothing in return, the act itself becomes more memorable. These memories, although great, actually fill up your memory bank and cause an emotional overload. I've seen it drive people to the point where they can neglect their family, neglect work, go without food, go with less sleep, and take the balance out of their lives.

Everyone is familiar with the term *workaholic*; well, this is a serve-aholic or volunteer-aholic. The situation where a person becomes consumed with helping other people is a real obsession that takes tremendous toll on physical and emotional wellness time and again. Such people reason that the work is never done, and they are constantly searching for a better way to make a difference.

Poverty and homelessness breed the greatest amounts of emotional response with their calls to arms, compared to the other social programs the United States government manages. The general public sees the government as a poor manager of these programs simply because the problem still exists in all fifty states. This area also creates the greatest amount of frustration because these conditions in individual cases can be reversed. The chronic poor or the destiny of poverty should not exist at all. The resources that our society currently enjoys certainly must be able to end the cycle of poverty. Yet no matter how hard we try, the problem still prevails. It seems like a country as great as ours would be capable of solving this problem in light of all the amazing accomplishments over the last century.

"POVERTY IS NOT A CONTACT SPORT! DON'T TOUCH IT! IT COULD SPREAD TO YOU!"

The biggest obstacle with poverty in the United States seems to be that most of us run away from the poor and homeless. Our government programs are falling short (the problem is too big for them) and poverty is a negative issue to the politicians. Talking about poverty and homelessness depresses people. Most politicians don't mention this topic as often as taxes, education, crime and world affairs. In addition, the very poor don't often go to the polls and the homeless don't go to the polls at all. Poverty is a problem that is stealth (odd that it rhymes with "wealth").

Poverty remains hidden in our country and the general public does not want to make contact with it. This issue may be the most important contribution to poverty in the United States. We simply do not want to make contact with the poor and homeless.

Society has always viewed poverty from the outside look-ing in. To view and study poverty is okay, but to live side-by-side with very poor people disgusts almost all Americans. The thought of building or buying a beautiful home that is next door to a home with peeling paint, broken or boarded windows, unmown lawns, rat-infested/bug infested/broken down construction and broken, rusty appliances really both-ers most people.

The history of poverty dates back to ancient writers who have given us a very specific account. Greece had dwell-ings with no heat in winter, no sanitary arrangements and no washing facilities. These accounts were described around 700 BC.[1]

In the Bible we learn how Joseph advised the Pharaoh of famine relief in ancient Egypt[2]

In a famine in Rome in 436 BC, thousands of starving people threw themselves into the Tiber. Even as these ter-rible examples were recorded, far fewer examples of the regular population helping the helpless were recorded. Pov-erty was treated as a normal lot! And poverty has been viewed as accepted in the development of the great societ-ies. Recurrent starvation continues through the whole of human history. The *Encyclopedia Britannica* lists thirty-one major famines ranging over 3000 years ("Famine" *Encyclo-pedia Britannica*). In a great famine in Bengal, ten million perished in 1709. France had over one million perish in the famine of 1769–70. France actually suffered eight fam-ines in the 18th century. In famines in Bombay, Madras and Mysore, five million perished. More recent famines in Biafra, Africa and Ethiopia are well known.

In the United States, of course, there is a striking differ-ence from the above facts. Mass starvation has never fallen on the United States, nor did it fall on any industrialized

Western country since the eighteenth century. The one exception may be the Irish Potato Famine in the 1800's. The problem in the United States is not mass starvation. Yet our internal poverty brings hunger, malnutrition, poor health care, alcoholism, drugs and early death.

Poverty as it stands today, and as it has stood for all time in history, is about lack of resources. This question can be brought up at this point: Is the problem a lack of distribution or a lack of production . . . or is it actually lack of access?

Are the poor really poor because something is being withheld from them, or are they incapable of producing enough to get by? If the poor could find a way to permanently increase their earnings, then poverty would be cured. However, it makes perfect sense to summarize that everyone would have their personal basic standard of living increased if they found a permanent way to increase earnings. We all face ups and downs. The factor which decides who is to be poor and who is going to be wealthy is that of opportunity.

Some people understand opportunity and how to capitalize on it. Others don't. How could a poor tribal Ethiopian farmer be capable of starting a high-tech company or a software company if he has never seen a computer in person? Could this person leapfrog over everyone else in the tribe and reach the point of becoming an entrepreneur or a captain of industry?

I have a friend who is now worth over one billion dollars. His story will demonstrate what I'm talking about. My friend called me on the telephone to describe how he had "hit it big." He went into details about the large venture partners and investors that were going to back his venture. I said, "Remember when you were so broke you couldn't pay your apartment rent and your truck was repossessed?" I told him, "You were poor back then." All of a sudden, he corrected me! He said, "Hey, I was never poor. I was broke . . . not poor. There is a big difference between the two."

He is right. There is a difference between being poor and being broke. Poor is permanent. Broke is temporary . . . temporarily out of money, or the politically correct language of "not liquid at this time," or better yet, "fiscally challenged."

The state of mind for my friend never changed, even when he was broke. He knew he was not poor. He wasn't raised poor. He doesn't have poor friends, and actually being poor was never an option for him. The biggest thing he knew was that he could always get a job. He was willing to live below his comfort level to make it to this higher level. He is much different from the "real poor." The real poor do have poor friends. The real poor were raised poor, their folks were poor, and everyone struggled—everyone around them. Are you all getting the picture yet? Everyone around them has always been poor. How could they break the cycle and rise above this without some kind of major change taking place? It is as much a state of mind as the reality itself. You see, the state of mind creates the reality!

The More Things Change, the More They Stay the Same.

Most of us baby-boomers remember the plight of the families in an area called Appalachia: parts of Kentucky, Tennessee, West Virginia, North Carolina and Virginia. This area experienced a high concentration of children going hungry and families living below the poverty level during the 1950s, the 1960s, and 1970s. The sad part is, that area is still in trouble. There are now 13.5 million children living at or below the poverty level in the United States. This is alarming because the situation is not getting better. The improvement that we all expected by the year 2000 has not materialized. Our kids are still going to bed hungry. In fact, one out of every FIVE kids in our country is hungry. This is pretty shameful when you also add the statistic that the U.S. ranks sixteenth in the world when it comes to efforts to raise children out of poverty.

Hunger may have a life of its own compared to poverty. These two things certainly go hand-in-hand, but there may be other reasons for hunger. In some cases pride takes over. One woman admitted that when people visit her home she makes sure they do not open her refrigerator. She is embarrassed to reveal that the refrigerator is mostly empty. Often food is not bought because rent must be paid. Many parents need every penny they make just to keep a roof over the head of family members. Either way, the parents are not about to admit to this because of pride and embarrassment. When the children do not have a hand in the decision on whether to buy food or pay rent, then these kids could be going to bed hungry more than the parents realize. Another sad fact may be that the children don't want to complain. Times may be too hard on their parents already.

With all the prosperity, where is the improvement? Well, the booming economy is actually hurting the poor. The fact that rents are skyrocketing might be keeping a decent place to live out of reach for many families. Housing and Urban Development recently reported a study which found that a record 5.4 million households spend more than half of their income on rent or are living in "severely distressed housing" and still rent is a major burden.

Can Our Government Create Opportunity?

The role of the United States government is in a very confusing situation. Should the government take substantial measures to eliminate poverty? If so, what should those measures be? Of course the real question becomes: How much would it cost?

The government has not solved the problem, and it may from time to time make the problem even worse. The expression "less is more" should guide our federal government. The government should do less to impede the free enterprise system. If anyone should be making contact with the poor, it should be the free enterprise system. The free enterprise system has the most resources and can deliver these resources faster than the federal government. The clearcut choice is that the private sector and people in their own communities are best suited for the job. So the question isn't what the government needs to do; it needs to get out of the way! Why? Because opportunity only comes from a free enterprise system.

The concept of investing with charity will be our best choice to lead the way. But charitable contributions will not be enough. It takes a lot of people and hands-on resources such as training, motivation, and frequent, consistent contact. Remember the story about the difference between the man who is given a fish and eats for one meal, and the man who is taught *how* to fish and eats for life. The problem with that story is, someone has to walk down to the creek with a fishing pole, take some bait, hooks and some extra fishing line in case it breaks, and he has to show the man how to fish, with encouragement and support until the lesson is learned.

It is the opinion of this author that the government and newer policies have created deterrence to taking on the challenges of the poor, the impoverished, and the have-nots. This is a policy in the use of "politically correct language." The why and the what-for are really quite obvious. It is the same principal behind motivating anyone to get off his or her duff to do something. Human behavior is complex, yet motivation is based on fear, greed, passion and love. Love and passion will not necessarily get the job done in a timely manner. Fear and greed will have a faster impact if you are looking for immediate results.

The point is, if we take the sense of urgency away from the fear factor or the greed factor, then we dilute a natural inclination to get things going. Children learn the sense of urgency based on the volume levels in their parents' voices. Raising one's voice is a natural response that we are all pretty much born with. Of course we are all taught to exercise control and refrain from verbal abuse in this process. Most of us can balance any anger we have within an acceptable range. Violence is always unacceptable and will produce the wrong results. Moderation today may be the most over emphasized aspect in today's society. Moderation is great, but with any behavior modification a price must be paid. The price paid in this case is effective results, directly related to someone's ability to effectively communicate. Without a sense of urgency within the process of communication, we will continue to see diminished response, extended time, and diluted motivation.

Professional public speakers know the reality of their listening audience and what makes for a memorable speech. These same principles will work in private conversation as well. The statistics on public speaking are that 15% of your effectiveness is in the content or words you actually use, and 30% of your effectiveness is based on how you delivered your message. This means: How good was the presentation? Did the speaker use visual aids? Did the speaker use an impressive vocabulary? Could he or she relate to the audience? The last principle, the one that has the most dramatic effect, around 50%, is appearance and behavior: How did the speaker look when the message was presented? Was the speaker relaxed, confident, well-dressed, well-groomed, firm, animated? Did he or she make eye contact, using effective gestures and so on? Professional speakers can use politically correct language because they maintain control of their audience. Remember most of them are paid speakers.

Contrary to the professional speaker, most of us are not as concerned about how we look when we speak to a close acquaintance or loved one; we are simply trying to get our point across quickly, and we are not being paid by the minute. Politically correct language takes the edge off reality, and research has shown it causes people to justify the wrong image. Politically correct language puts love and compassion back into the language itself. This seems nice and it is nice, but the purpose of any language is to objectively communicate. This use of this abatement of the English language is wrong and will hurt us in the long run .I list some examples that we have all heard and thought about, which place compassion into the language but also diminish and take the edge off everyday realities:

1. Someone is a bad or violent child.	1. Someone is A.D.D. and A.D.H.D.
2. Someone is serving prison time.	2. Someone is residing in a correctional facility.
3. Someone is blind.	3. Someone is vision-impaired.
4. Someone is lazy.	4. Someone is motivationally challenged.
5. Someone is homosexual.	5. Someone has come out of the closet.

| 6. Someone is poor. | 6. Someone is underprivileged. |
| 7. Someone is late. | 7. Someone has a new arrival time. |

On the above list we see the word "underprivileged." This is such a broad-based word it could not describe a specific problem. It would be difficult for all of us to conclude exactly what area of underprivileged someone might be referring to.

Perhaps honesty in America may solve the problem of poverty. There are some encouraging statistics; the United States economy is strong and millionaires are being created faster than ever before. The impact of all this may not be felt immediately, but over time it could make a measurable difference. The shift in new wealth should be accompanied by a shift to "Let's get our hands dirty" or "Let's get to work." Is it more important to give money to charity or is it more important to have met the person you wish to help, and help them carry a fishing pole to catch their own food? Charity is about giving, but it is also about serving. As a nation, and more importantly, as a community, we must smash the barriers that deter us from helping each other. This definitely has to do with community. "I want to help the poor, I just don't want to live near them." Isolating the problem is the problem.

The second example of reality we need to address as a nation is our track record with the impoverished. I researched the practice of moving the poor. The following descriptions seem to exemplify the alienation of the poor and homeless, and, if continued, would keep them isolated. Here are the four terms used and their definitions:

Gentrification—The purposeful transformation of a neighborhood into an area that will attract higher income residents through displacement of lower income tenants. Examples are recent renovation, upscale businesses and upscale retail stores.

Greyhound Therapy—This was the practice of providing one-way, out-of-town bus tickets to homeless or others seeking shelter and benefits, such as newly discharged mental patients or recently paroled prisoners.

NIMBY—(Not In My Back Yard) is a term used against programs that aid the undesirable, such as homeless shelters, prisons, waste sites These are typically ballot measures, which are decided by the voters.

Magnet Theory—This idea can be proposed by public officials or by residents who are opposed to measures that assist the homeless in their community. The premise is that the availability of services will attract homeless or poor from other areas, which is undesirable.

What do these really say in our society? They all say, "I'd rather see someone else deal with the problem." It also says we may be all for creating opportunity, but only for the people who will make our community attractive. The unattractive need to move somewhere else.

Poverty in America is desperate and sad, but it is not at epic proportions. In fact, it has been, and still is, isolated. The worst proportion of cases of homeless people exists in Boston and Washington, D.C., at an estimated 35 to 50 persons per 10,000. The rest of the country averages around 10 homeless per 10,000 in the rest of the U.S. cities (Burt & Cohen, pg. 23). The poverty line in the United States today is $8,350 per individual, $17,050 for a family of four (as previously discussed in chapter 2). These amounts are astronomical compared to the rest of the world, where dollar figures are much lower (*Federal Register*, pg. 2). Most non-Western countries do not keep statistics on their homeless and poor because it is too impossible to count.

The government alone will not solve the problem. The new wealth combined with charitable giving *will* solve the problem. The problem must first be dealt with head-on, without disgust, and without a NIMBY attitude.

Community is the answer, and acceptance of the problem, with resources backing the effort, will work. I am not saying that all people have the same motivation, nor do they have the same skills. I do believe that our quest for community can make a difference if we don't run away or push people aside. We won't be able to make the unattractive fit into the beautiful neighborhoods. Isolation is not the answer, so we must seek an idea that fulfills acceptance.

We have been laboring under the misconception that the strong will rule the weak forever. Social Darwinism has destroyed the interplay between humankind. Social Darwinism has had its day. We should no longer ask, "What is the world coming to?" We need to know what's coming to the world! You will soon have the ability to see a starving child in Africa on a live video satellite picture on your computer. People will no longer sit back and say, "I wish there was something I could do about the poor child." Very soon the technology will exist that could locate and provide food and supplies to that child within hours. These facts will be bigger than the Internet. These new technological advancements will truly have an impact in ways that the world has only dreamed about.

The next *new* new thing will bring us together and support our dreams for all mankind. For those suffering from an identity crisis or just trying to figure out the importance of it all, I give the following advice: There is something better than telling people how important you are, and that is having people tell others how important you made them feel.

> "My responsibility is to get my twenty-five guys playing for the name on the front of their uniform and not the name on the back."
>
> —Tommy Lasorda

❧ *Chapter Four* ☙

THE DIFFERENCE BETWEEN FINANCIAL CAPITAL & SOCIAL CAPITAL

I begin with the premise that two things will come to pass in my lifetime: (1) that as United States citizens we will eventually become *world* citizens living within our country, and (2) that it will become more exciting to give our money away than it was actually making that money. This second premise is really what makes the difference between social capital and financial capital and their respective meanings.

Winston Churchill said it best: "We make a living by what we get; we make a life by what we give." Your financial capital is "what you get." Your social capital is "what you give." Having money is success. Giving generously is significance!

Winston Churchill probably understood the concept of "world charity" back in the 1940's. His words help us begin to understand that "stewardship is not an option." Winston Churchill saw many countries pool their resources to fight against Hitler's evil regime. That was a time when people helped people or they were going to be conquered, imprisoned or exterminated. The dominant ruled the weak, and only through man's compassion toward fellow man were acts of charity and sacrifice pushed to the limits during World War II.

One of the first Biblical acts of charitable giving was discussed in Ezra 3:6–7: "On the first day of the seventh month they began to offer burnt offerings to the Lord, though the foundation of the Lord's temple had not been laid. Then they gave money to the masons and carpenters, and gave food and drink and oil to the people of Sidon and Tyre."

The people came together in this story to rebuild the temple and to rebuild the altar, which was destroyed by King Zedekiah. The book of Ezra also gives accounts of the "neighbors" bringing silver, gold, goods and livestock to the temple. "When they arrived at the house of the Lord in Jerusalem, some of the heads of the families gave freewill offerings toward the rebuilding of the house of God on its site. According to their ability they gave the treasury for this work 61,000 drachmas of gold, 5000 minas of silver and 100 priestly garments" (Ezra 3:68).

Back in those days, things were pretty cut and dried. Stewardship, charity and sacrifice were not options. Basically, if someone was greedy and did not follow charitable doctrine from the priests and leaders, then they risked grave consequences.

The new philanthropy is evolving in ways that we are only now beginning to understand. The trend in philanthropy is attributed to a new emergence of philanthropists. This means it is an exciting time because there is more new wealth than ever before. We are seeing people who have built fortunes in months, as opposed to over a lifetime.

Therefore, it would be logical to state that giving has reached another level of truly significant height. The computer geeks and nerds, the dot.com billionaires, all are looking at their social capital. Their new capital for making a difference will be significant, but nothing is cut and dried. The Internet took a lot of time to build, and tremendous brainpower has been harnessed in order to deliver the results we now enjoy. Charitable fulfillment must go through the same process. Building a charitable Internet can be done, but it must undergo a process of understanding.

Success = Intellectual Capital
Fear + Greed = Financial Capital
Feeling: Satisfied, Significant or Spontaneous = Social Capital

The way we can build our charitable Internet will be with the combination of all three factors. One could argue about these all working together toward the same goal. Let's view the arguments. Intellectual capital is how we became successful. An idea put in place with a working plan will produce a successful project. Financial capital is pointing in the direction of growth and leverage opportunities. Social capital is about giving money away and I might add, giving it away without any conditions attached. Unless our tax laws change, the definition of a charitable gift is one that is given with no conditions attached, and the donor should expect nothing in return. Otherwise a gift becomes non-deductible. Foundations and charities, on the other hand, are supposed to be good stewards of the capital. Their job should strive to leverage and multiply the activity. An activity or charity that doesn't expand and reach out to more recipients is viewed as not fulfilling the mission. Everyone expects results. Look at what the Internet has done. Shouldn't we ask why charity can't do the same?

There is a difference between financial capital and social capital, yet knowing the difference is not important. What is important is how to improve and take advantage of both your financial capital and your social capital at the same time. A strategic plan for both is a must. This is where intellectual capital takes over.

The definition of capital is "money." In order to get money and keep money, you must first understand the four P's, four planning techniques that will increase financial capital and social capital. They are:

1. Investment PLANNING
2. Insurance PLANNING
3. Retirement PLANNING
4. Estate PLANNING

There are no two ways about it. One must utilize all four of these or a huge percentage of wealth will be lost due to taxes, poor money management, accidents, sickness and untimely deaths.

THE FIRST "P"

Investment Planning has so many clichés. "It is not what you make, it's what you keep that counts." Or, "Most people don't plan to fail, they fail to plan." Or, "The average American family spends more time planning a family vacation than they spend on their investment planning." The tools available in the areas of tracking investment returns, real-time stock quotes, and free access to professional advice by media and internet is nothing short of amazing. It is a wonder why we're not all multi-millionaires. Of course a lot of us are actually in this category. As of the writing of this book, sixty-six millionaires are created each day between the cities of San Jose, California and San Francisco, California. In case you're unfamiliar with the geography, those cities are about forty-one miles apart. Another interesting fact is that the fastest growing categories of family incomes are those making over one million dollars per year.

The biggest concept that people must grasp is that it requires capital to do any investment planning. In other words, investors must be savers before they become investors. Yes, you can borrow to invest, but you'd better make sure you're "on the mark" most all of the time.

In order to be efficient in investment planning, one must understand that there are different asset categories and they will have cycles and vary in performance. The stock market has been the best game in town for the last nineteen years. When I was doing an investment seminar a few years back, I asked the audience a question: What, in your opinion, was the best single investment ever made throughout the history of the United States? How about the Louisiana Purchase for $17 million . . . or Alaska for $2.00 per acre . . . or best of all, the entire island of Manhattan for $24, purchased from the American Indians in 1626?

Well, interestingly enough (and I hate it when I think of those Native American ancestors who have been deprived), if they had invested that money (7% over inflation rate) since 1626, then that mere $24 would be worth $100 trillion dollars today, based on compound interest! That would buy all the real estate in the United States as well as the cities of London, Paris and Tokyo. I would like to point out that it would be that much if it were in a tax-free foundation. Outside of a foundation and in today's top tax bracket, it would be worth only $900 million. Taxes are very devastating to compound interest.

That would have been proper investment planning on behalf of the Native Americans, if they had invested that $24 and turned it into ownership of all the real estate in the United States plus London, Paris and Tokyo. These seem like incredible returns, yet to me what has occurred in the last five years is much more incredible. Forget about a 7% return after inflation is taken out. How about 7000% returns that have been achieved by companies and investors in twelve months? Qualcomm can lay claim to this. Investment planning must be flexible and strategic to fit your age, your risk tolerance and your life plans and obligations.

THE SECOND "P"

Insurance Planning is about protection from loss. To say that insurance is an offensive tactic is a stretch. Insurance is a defensive strategy that can keep and protect a lot of assets. The effective use of the life insurance trust as a way for heirs to pay off inheritance and estate tax will be discussed later in this book. One such advantage is that, for a number of historical reasons in connection with the purposes of life insurance, it is not unusual for significant *creditor protection* statutory or case law authority to be provided for such policies under local law in the United States and elsewhere. This type of protection often extends to the lifetime benefits as well as to the death proceeds under these contracts.

One often-overlooked advantage of life insurance is that, because of its unusual confidentiality, it allows a family patriarch or matriarch to quietly make financial "adjustments" within a family unit (whether or not a closely-held business is involved) in order to avoid conflict because of perhaps pre-existing cultural prejudices or other reasons. Understanding life insurance and its uses could truly become the modern-day Robin Hood. Rob from the rich (the tax man/IRS), and give back to the poor.

THE THIRD "P"

Retirement Planning is a balancing act between taxes and compound interest. It is best to begin with compound interest, which is based on the Rule of 72. The Rule of 72 is a method used to determine how long it will take to double your money at a particular interest rate. It states that your money will double at a point in time by dividing 72 by the interest earned. For example: By earning 7.2% rate of return, you will double your money in ten years.

72 ÷ 7.2 % interest or earnings rate = 10 years.

The other formula can determine what interest rate you'll need to double your money within a certain time. This other formula can calculate the rate of interest you'll need for a special time period by dividing 72 by the number of years your are investing.

72 ÷ 10 years = 7.2% interest rate.

Let's try two more equations:

72 ÷ 4.2% interest rate = 17 years to double your money.
72 ÷ 17 years = 4.2% interest rate.

The next challenge to retirement planning is taxes. Remember the government will tax you when you make money and when you save money.

I try to impress on people the time value of money. When you give your money more time to accumulate, the earnings on your investments—and the annual compounding of those earnings—can make a big difference in your final return.

Consider a hypothetical investor who saved $2,000 per year for ten years, then didn't add to her next egg for the next ten years. She has $67,500 after twenty years, assuming she earned 8% annually in a tax-deferred account.

Another investor waited ten years, then tried to make up for lost time by investing $4,000 annually for the next ten years. Even though he invests more, $40,000 versus the early bird's $20,000, he still ends up with a smaller next egg. Assuming he too earns 8% per year, his final account value is only $62,581. Most of the procrastinator's nest egg, 63%, is the principal he invested. The majority of the early bird's account, 70%, is earnings.

Don't count on Social Security. When protecting sources of income in retirement, I discount Social Security if the person is under age 50. It's not that I think the program will go away. I just don't think it will be available in its current form when people under 50 are ready to retire. My wife and I aren't expecting to receive Social Security. We know it could be "means tested' when we retire. With means testing, benefits would be tied to retirees' financial needs. Those with incomes above certain limits might be given defined benefits—similar to a defined benefit pension plan.

Understanding Social Capital

Social Capital may have a broad definition, but for you and your family it can be as personal as it gets. The ability to direct the success of your passion will take some major planning, as well.

Understanding the forms of capital—financial capital and social capital—that comprise wealth also should increase charitable motivation. Financial capital, or capital owned by individuals, and social capital, or capital owned by society, is used to create three types of social capital, which can be described as:

1. Government-controlled social capital that comes from taxes.
2. Charity-controlled social capital that comes from charitable contributions.
3. Family-controlled social capital that comes from the funding of family charities.

Perhaps more wealthy individuals would choose to fund charity-controlled social capital and family-controlled social capital if they were aware of the choices available. Wealthy individuals could be encouraged to have a greater influence on their communities if they better understood the potential power and magnitude of the social capital at their disposal.

Old or established wealth has a tradition of providing inheritances for children and using trusts to accomplish the twin goals of minimizing transfer taxes and controlling the inheritance. Conversely, new wealth views the acquisition of wealth as a measure of one's success and achievement and believes wealth must be newly earned by each generation rather than inherited. To new money, nothing outclasses achievement. Observing how inheriting great wealth can corrupt young people, a conclusion was made that inherited wealth can be a curse as well as a blessing.

On the other hand, a reluctance to transfer large inheritances to children does not mean that parents are not concerned with providing for their children's basic needs. Devising ways to meet those needs requires estate and trust planning to accommodate unexpected expenses associated with disability of a child and other emergency expenses, in addition to providing for items categorized as basic needs such as education, start-up capital for a business, and capital for the purchase of a home.

Two well-known billionaires illustrate the new approach to inheritance. Microsoft founder Bill Gates (age 42) has said that he will give $10 million each to his baby daughter, Jennifer, and her future siblings, with the rest going to charity. Warren Buffett (age 66) has been less specific about how much his three children should expect—figures of $1 million to $10 million each have appeared in the media. Many wealthy individuals with smaller estates share the views of Gates and Buffett, planning a limited albeit generous inheritance for their heirs.

When new wealth individuals prioritize charitable gifting over family gifting, a logical question they must consider is how to accomplish this wisely. "Virtual Philanthropy" is a new buzz-phrase sweeping the country with our dot-com friends. These givers claim to be hands-on, with charitable causes all sorted out as to who gets what. Venture philanthropy should take a back seat to leveraged gifting strategies and to giving with pre-tax dollars. The extra money that would be going toward the needy will make a greater impact in the long run.

Remember, in the "football game of life" you need the right team on the field to maximize your social capital. In the football game of life the score should be:

GIVERS	NON-GIVERS
100	0

We're in the 4th Quarter. Any questions?

❧ Chapter Five ❧

THE FAMILY FOUNDATION:
A Blessing or a Curse?

"I highly recommend that people do not GIVE to charity. Instead, I strongly recommend that people INVEST IN or WITH a charity!"

The best way to invest in charity is for the donor to "be" the charity or to exercise a level of control that can equate to the same satisfaction as they receive from growth or positive results that happen in everyday business or personal activities.

The current IRS rules prohibit donors from receiving or deriving a direct economic benefit from a tax-deductible gift. If a donor gives a gift and receives something back of any value, then the IRS considers this transaction "self-dealing." However, the New Charity is about expanding the gift, multiplying the gift, and utilizing the gift in a manner that gives something back to the donor's family members. When this strategy is executed properly, then the amount donated is no longer a "gift." Instead, it becomes an "investment" in philanthropic terms. Investments are good things to be involved with, and to be able to have a say in the decisions is also a very good way to serve the individual passions that are "dear to one's heart."

Setting up a Family Foundation

What is the definition of overkill? Forming and maintaining your own private family foundation. Just knowing the IRS rules would keep you up at night. Those rules also work well if you have trouble sleeping. Begin reading those rules at about 10 p.m. and you'll go right to sleep!

Actually, the foundation as parking lot for your social capital is the way to go. The IRS just took the fun out of it by putting too many restrictions on the compliance issues. Legal professionals of your choosing should explore the family foundation, its intentions, its legal structure and its alternative. It is an important decision. This chapter will attempt to enlighten you regarding certain features, benefits and pitfalls regarding what is best for your family legacy planning. It is, however, not a complete process for your understanding without the advice of outside legal professionals.

Family Foundations. The most common type of private foundation is generally referred to as a family foundation, or standard private foundation. "Family foundation" is not a legal term, but denotes those private foundations created by, funded by, usually named after, and controlled by an individual or family. It is estimated that about two-thirds of the foundations in the United States are family foundations. Ranging in asset size from a few hundred thousand dollars to hundreds of millions of dollars, family foundations as a whole hold an estimated $86 billion in assets and make grants of around $5 billion per year. However, the majority have assets of less than $5 million. Most family foundations are run by family members who serve as trustees or directors on a voluntary basis, receiving no compensation. In many cases, second-and-third generation descendants of the original donors manage the foundations.

Funds usually are received only from one individual, family, or corporation. Family foundations do not, for the most part, get involved in fundraising and do not themselves apply for grants. The family foundation suffers the entire excise tax regimen that the Revenue Code offers up. These excise taxes can amount to twenty-seven different categories of tax. Most family foundations concentrate their giving in their local communities.

Advantages of Creating a Private Foundation

Control. The main advantage of a private foundation over the alternatives is control. Because most successful entrepreneurs have a distinct aversion to loss of control, the control inherent in the use of a private foundation for family philanthropy is attractive.

When an individual creates and contributes to a private foundation during life, he or she is able to take an income tax deduction immediately, but may continue to control the distribution of the foundation's assets to charitable organizations in the future.

Family Name Recognition. Many foundations carry the family name of the founder—a way to perpetuate the founder's name as the foundation lives on and does good works for the community. A family foundation preserves a family's wealth and perpetuates its influence and memory better than almost any other form of legacy.

Establishing a foundation demonstrates to a community that the family is committed to philanthropy. The family has money that it must give away, which encourages community charities to approach the foundation for grants. Through designing and following a strategic giving plan, the foundation's board can ensure that grants are awarded to organizations that will uphold the foundation's goals for community improvement.

Influence. A family foundation can wield substantial influence to improve the quality of the giving itself and its intent.

Family Values Perpetuation. The experience of serving on the foundation board or a committee can be a powerful vehicle for transmitting the founding family values to younger generations. Young family members can assume responsibility for areas appropriate for their education and ability. Foundation governance meetings focus on administration and operation of the foundation, along with discussions regarding grants to be made, reports from charities who have received grants, and reports from members on charities being considered for future grants. The common goals and purpose of the foundation can serve to unite family members in ways they have not previously experienced, a family benefit that in today's world may be one of the most important benefits to the foundation's founder.

Disadvantages of Creating a Private Foundation

In order for a private foundation to fulfill its purpose it must have income. Private foundations do not solicit funds. If they were to solicit funds they would not be private, they would be public. This raises the question of how a private foundation is funded. The National Council on Foundations provides a description of private foundations that clarifies some points: "Occasionally in the form of a trust, but usually organized as a non-profit corporation the independent foundation is the most common type of private foundation. Sometimes referred to as a 'family foundation.'" Because it usually does not directly operate any charitable service or activity, it is sometimes called a private non-operating foundation.

Another disadvantage of the family foundation is the lack of creditor protection versus a full-blown 501(c)(3) charity. A lawsuit can pierce the corporate veil, so to speak, and the family can be directly liable for any mistakes or abuses through oversight or lack of attention.

Private foundations have mandatory minimum distribution requirements. (The precise description of these requirements is covered in IRS 4942(d), IRS 4942(e), IRS 514(1), Joint Committee on Internal Revenue Taxation, General Explanation of Tax Reform Act of 1969, 91st Cong. 2d Sess. At 36; also Rev. Rul. 67–5 C.B. 123. The mandatory distribution requirements for private foundations can be summarized by "the 5 percent pay-out rule." The rule applies to the fair market value of all the assets of the private foundation, other than those being used or held for use in directly carrying out the private foundation's tax-exempt purpose.

The assets that are generally used or held for use for tax-exempt purposes include, but are not limited to, any interest in a functionally related business or in a program related investment.

In simpler terms, a minimum of 5 percent of the contributions received and income earned in a year must be paid out to a public or private charity or charities. It is best to leave the computations for exact minimum payout requirements to the accountants. However, it turns out that the average payout from private foundations exceeds the minimum requirement by a significant margin. The IRS can levy

27 different excise taxes on a private foundation, which can be a major headache. This also reveals that private foundations are not really tax-exempt. There is going to be an actual tax charged against the foundation each year.

The concepts discussed in this book, while they may not be widely known, are certainly not secret, obscure or arcane. What has been presented is fact based on law, tax code and widely accepted practice. We see that an estate organized in trust form, in certain areas, falls under a distinct set of laws the result of which may be advantageous to the estate. There are a large percentage of individuals, professionals and practitioners that are unfamiliar with these concepts and laws regarding them. The facts are readily available to anyone who wishes to familiarize himself with them.

Tax Deductibility of Contributions to Private Foundations

Contributions to private foundations are subject to a number of restrictions on income tax deductibility, as set forth in Section 170 of the Internal Revenue Code ("Code"). Cash contributions are generally deductible up to 30 percent of a donor's adjusted gross income (AGI), while contributions of appreciated property are typically deductible up to only 20 percent of the donor's AGI. If the 20 percent and 30 percent limitations are exceeded, excess deductions may be carried forward for five years. The limitations on deductibility for contributions to private foundations are less generous than those applicable to contributions to public charities. A cash contribution to a public charity is deductible up to 50 percent of a donor's AGI, and a donor may deduct contributions of appreciated property to a public charity of up to 30 percent of his or her AGI.

Previously, up until May 31, 1998, donors were permitted to deduct the full fair market value (up to their maximum percentage limitations) of gifts to a private foundation of qualified appreciated stock, when:

- The market quotations for the stock are available on an established securities market.
- The stock is capital gain property in the hands of the donor.
- The stock is in a company of which the donor and his or her family have contributed less than 10 percent in value, counting prior contributions.

This provision has been extended permanently.

THE DONOR ADVISED ACCOUNT

I call this *My Charity*. A donor advised account is like having your own private charity that can serve like a public charity. The advantages are numerous over a private foundation because basically this account sits under a Master Foundation. The Master Foundation is responsible for doing the administration, reporting, and accounting and compliance issues. A donor advised account is a very good vehicle for philanthropy. The donor has the potential for great diversification in the actual placement of gifts. This is an advantage over the private foundation, whose limitations may include restrictions on the recipients of its gifts.

The Donor Advised Account (DAA) is a family foundation that has all the benefits of a larger public charity. It provides the donor an opportunity to make a difference by using their passion with flexibility of timing and specific causes. Historically, the Donor Advised Account dates back to 1914 when the Cleveland Foundation first used it. This foundation placed itself under a religious organization at that time, and it has continued for over 85 years.

Why the Donor Advised Account?

You can:
1. Convert a life of success into a life of significance.
2. Fund your specific passion with creative use of assets.
3. Provide a platform for the family to work together, sorting out their charitable priorities.
4. Educate younger members of the family on the importance of giving.
5. Create a legacy that can be passed on and managed by each maturing family member.

Should you start a Donor Advised Account?

Yes, if:
*   You would like your choice to decide where and when to donate, sent directly to charities in *your own foundation's name*.
*   You would like to take *a tax deduction* in the year you make your gift, but decide later which charities will receive the money.
*   You desire to make a tax-free gift now, and *earn interest tax-free* on that amount over time, so you can have more money to give later on.
*   You are doing a Charitable Gifting Strategy such as a Charitable Remainder Trust or Charitable Gift Annuity, and you wish to have the *remaining interest go to the causes you support*.

- You have a specific purpose and want to make it possible for more than one person to donate and *receive tax deductions*.
- You wish to avoid the necessary record keeping and quarterly status reports, which will be provided *free-of-charge* by a group such as Charitable Alliance Foundation.

These are the Rules

- You may give to any IRS-recognized *public* benefit, charity, church, or school.
- You *can't* give to a non-charity, or a foreign charity not registered with the IRS.
- You *can't* give in a way that confers a benefit to you or your family. For example, you **can't** make a gift to your child's school that goes to pay your child's tuition. But you **can** make a gift to fund scholarships for deserving students selected by the school.
- You *can't* leave funds in your account for an indefinite, unreasonable period without naming the charity(s) that will ultimately benefit.
- As funds are deposited in your foundation account, you can make gift distributions at any time by communicating your instructions to Charitable Alliance Foundation *in writing* (mail or fax).

These are the Benefits

- **A simple, flexible and cost-effective way to make gifts**. You can use the account to make one gift or a series of gifts. You may choose charities at your own pace and maintain flexibility with your giving program. You can *receive many of the benefits* of a private foundation with fewer complexities and lower cost.
- **Better tax planning.**

Your tax deduction is effective on the day your gift is accepted by the account. If you need to lock in tax deductions late in the year, you can do so with confidence, and without having to evaluate many charities and their needs.

- **Flexible planning for charitable giving.**
Other people may make gifts to be included in an account you establish. *They would receive tax deductions*, and your recommended charities would be considered for grants. For instance, you could set up a scholarship fund at an educational institution and all your family and friends might contribute to it.

- **Capital gains tax relief on appreciated securities.**
You may make gifts of appreciated securities (such as stocks or mutual fund shares) directly to the account and thereby *avoid paying capital gains tax,* **which would be due upon a sale. In addition, any future appreciation on these securities** *will not be taxable* **to you or included in your estate.**

- **Professional investment management.**
The account's assets are invested in diversified, professionally managed portfolios. This means that you may *set assets aside for future disbursement* **to charity without having to manage those assets yourself or hire an investment manager.**

- **Low cost.**
Avoids outside legal fees. Donors who make gifts to the account are not billed for any of the Fund's services. The Fund pays the trustee a percentage on each deposit for administrative services. The only other Fund expenses are investment management fees.

- **Full administration and reporting.**

The account provides all the administrative and reporting services you need for a giving program, including the documentation you need to calculate and support income tax deductions.

DONOR ADVISED ACCOUNT VS. PRIVATE FOUNDATION

INDIVIDUAL DONOR ACCOUNT	PRIVATE FOUNDATION
• Low cost start-up. • No attorney fees. • Low funding requirements • Low minimum to start funding • Records are not public	• Costly start-up and legal fees. • Costly accounting and maintenance fees. • Most foundations start in the $1/2 million range. • Tax return is public record Form 990PF
• Can have the account under (your name) Family Foundation and solicit volunteers, fundraising, etc.	• Excise tax assessed on Private Foundations of 2% on annual income, and restrictions on gifting.
• No annual distribution requirement. Can hold funds.	• Must give out at least 5% per year.
• Greater income tax deductions allowed: • 50% of AGI for cash gift. • 30% of appreciated securities.	• Smaller income tax deductions: • 30% of AGI for cash. • 20% of AGI for appreciated assets.

Last, but not least . . . while a Donor Advised Account can grow tax-free, the donor can consider a conversion later to a Private Foundation, from which heirs could derive salaries and expenses paid to them in perpetuity. These salaries must be within reason; however, an active foundation would justify paying higher salaries if the job is more than part time. Abuses in this area can occur, yet I have found the regulators rarely enforce restrictions on salaries if charitable activities are the purpose of the salary. The key element is the good you are doing and the ability to put in significant amounts of work.

❧ *Chapter Six* ❧

PLANNED GIVING

I n many ways, this is an oxymoron. How can we, or how should we plan our passion? Shouldn't our giving be spontaneous and from the heart? The problem is, that is exactly the wrong thing for charity! Charitable needs just keep coming and the needs become constant. A charity cannot rely on impulse giving. It can't afford to hold its breath while donors get motivated by compassion.

Planned giving is about establishing a pipeline. Planned giving must be viewed through the eyes of the charity rather than the donor. The donor desires to feel spontaneous; the charity desires to feel secure with a reliable source of capital or a large endowment. Bill Wilson, pastor of Metro Ministries, Brooklyn, New York, said it best: "I don't care about planned giving. I care about planned getting, to help my kids." Bill Wilson runs the largest Sunday school in the world. 40,000 children go to his church every Sunday in Brooklyn, New York.

In a previous chapter I mentioned the definition of insanity, which is doing the same thing over and over, yet expecting a different result. The motto, however, must be: One step back, two steps forward. Everything works in fundraising and nothing works. It all depends on timing, circumstances (such as the economy), what's in the news, and other such factors. When some event like the tragedy at Columbine High School occurs, then people will be receptive. Unfortunately, much like life, charitable needs move forward slowly, and focusing on knee-jerk campaigns will be quite unsuccessful over the long run.

In this chapter you will learn about "planned getting techniques" that can make a dramatic impact to a needy cause. These are not to be construed as the one and only method available. However, these are win-win situations for donor and charity. These techniques are: the Charitable Lead Trust, the Charitable Gift Annuity, the Charitable Remainder Trust, and using a Charitable Gift Annuity with a Family Foundation Donor Advised Account.

THE CHARITABLE LEAD TRUST

You Can Lead a Horse to Water, but Your Church or Charity Needs a "Lead Trust"

The win-win for donor and charity can be the Charitable Lead Trust Account. If the objective of the family is to shield more of your accumulated wealth from gift and estate taxes, and you are interested in providing support to your favorite charity, then the Lead Trust may be for you.

Remember, property passing from parents to heirs can be taxed up to 55%. That tax is imposed at the death of the last spouse and is due in nine (9) months. Your children may receive only $450,000 of each $1,000,000 in your estate.

Why does a Lead Trust save large amounts of estate and gift taxes?

When a lead trust is created, only the present value of the remainder interest (the amount remaining for your heirs when the trust terminates) will be subject to tax.

> **Example:** Ernie funds a lead trust with $1,000,000 and stipulates that the church is to receive $80,000 per year for 15 years, after which the remaining principal will be distributed to his two children. He will report a taxable gift of only $223,020. The difference ($1,000,000 - $223,020 = $776,980) is a gift-tax charitable deduction. If he had simply given the $1,000,000 to his children, the entire amount would have been taxable.

Under this plan you would irrevocably transfer assets to a trustee and provide that payments be made to the charity for a certain number of years (or until the end of your or another's life). Then the principal would be distributed to your children, grandchildren, or other heirs. The principal passes to your heirs at greatly reduced gift-and-estate-tax rates, and sometimes escapes them altogether.

When can a Lead Trust be established?

A lead trust can be established either during your lifetime or under your will. Creating it during your life and designating the remainder for heirs results in a *gift-tax deduction*. Creating it by will produces an *estate-tax deduction*.

What determines the size of the charitable deduction?

Three factors affect the deduction: (1) the duration of the trust; (2) the amount paid to the charity each year; and (3) the federal discount rate in effect when the trust is established. Lengthening the trust term and enlarging the payments to the charity will increase the deduction.

A lower federal discount rate also increases the charitable deduction. As that rate drops, lead trusts become more appealing. Those who establish a lead trust now can obtain a significant deduction without having to postpone distributions to heirs as long as they might have when rates were higher.

Will a Lead Trust also save income tax?

You receive an income-tax deduction only if the principal will be returned to you at the termination of the trust or if you have retained some other power over the trust causing you to be treated as the owner. The cost for obtaining this deduction is that you are taxed on the payments to the charity even though you are not receiving them. If you expect your income-tax bracket to drop, it may be advantageous to have an up-front deduction when your rate is high and then be taxed on the income when your rate is lower. However, this is a rather uncommon use of the lead trust. Most people do not have the principal returned to them but rather distributed to heirs. They retain no personal financial interest in their trusts and, thus, are not treated as owners. While they receive no income-tax deductions, they are not taxed on the payments to the charity. They also are able to get the property into the hands of heirs at the lowest possible gift-and-estate-tax rates.

How long will payments be made?

The payment period to the charity is at your choosing, subject only to the rule against perpetuities applicable in some states. Most lead trusts last for a term of years, but the trust could also extend for the duration of your or another's life.

Other factors in your decision may be the current ages of your children or grandchildren, when they would be mature enough to manage the property, and the length of time and amount of money you want to place in support of the charity's programs. Also, you might choose a trust term that will result in no transfer tax or will at least produce the deduction required for your estate plan.

How are the payments to the charity determined?

If the trust is to qualify for a charitable deduction, the payments must be a fixed dollar amount (charitable lead annuity trust) or a fixed percentage of the trust assets as determined annually (charitable lead unitrust).

Example of charitable lead annuity trust: John transfers $1,000,000 and stipulates that the charity is to receive $70,000 per year for the duration of the trust. If the trust earns more than $70,000, the excess will be added to the principal and accumulated for heirs. If it earns less than $70,000, the principal will be invaded to make the required payment, thereby diminishing the amount left for heirs.

Example of charitable lead unitrust: Joanna transfers $1,000,000 and stipulates that the charity is to receive 7% of the net fair-market value of the trust assets as determined annually. If the value of the trust property increases to $1,100,000 by the beginning of the third year, the charity would be paid $77,000 that year. Conversely, if the value of the trust property fell to $900,000, the charity would receive $63,000. As with the annuity trust, the principal is invaded if necessary to make the required payments.

Payments must be determined in either of these two ways. A trust that simply pays net income to charity, whatever it may be, will not qualify for tax benefits.

Which method of determining payments is better?

If you believe the property will appreciate in value, and you would like your heirs to benefit from the growth, then a charitable lead annuity trust is preferable.

> *Example: Sam's $1,000,000 contribution consists of growth stock with a total net return (including appreciation) of 12% per year. The stock funds a 15-year charitable lead annuity trust that pays $80,000 per year to the charity. When the trust terminates, the principal will have grown to $2,491,189.*

If Sam had transferred the stock to a charitable lead unitrust instead, the principal distributed to his heirs would have been $1,800,944—nearly $700,000 less. Of course, the charity would have received considerably more. Since the charity receives a percentage of trust assets as valued each year, the charity shares in the growth. With the charitable lead annuity trust, on the other hand, the payments to the charity are held at a fixed level. All appreciation is accumulated for heirs. If the trust's total return had been less than 8%, the heirs would have fared better with a charitable lead unitrust.

Is capital gain subject to tax?

If the trust holds property that appreciates and then distributes that property to your heirs, the gain will not be subject to gift or estate taxes. Suppose, for example, that the property was worth $1,000,000 when you created the trust, $700,000 of that amount was deductible, and the property's value will have increased to $3,000,000 by the time the trust ends. Your heirs will receive $3,000,000, but you will have paid gift or estate taxes on a mere $300,000—which is why the lead trust is so appealing if you want to transfer an asset you expect to keep increasing in value.

> *Note: When your heirs sell the property, they will be taxed on the capital gain. Their basis will be the value of the property at the time of your death if the trust was funded under your will. If you created the trust during your lifetime, they will take over your basis.*

Possibly the trust will sell part of the property, use some of the proceeds to make the payments to the charity, and reinvest the balance. In this case the trust will be taxed on the gain, though it may deduct the amount paid to a charity.

What kinds of property may be transferred?

Cash, publicly traded securities, closely held stock, and real estate are all acceptable for charitable lead trusts. Ideally, the property will generate enough income to make the payments to charity. If not, assets will have to be sold. You will maximize the tax benefits if you transfer property with good growth potential.

Can my grandchildren, rather than my children, be beneficiaries of a lead trust?

Yes, you may name whomever you wish. However, when you skip a generation, the generation-skipping tax may be imposed. Each individual is allowed a $1,000,000 exemption ($1,030,000 for 2000, indexed for inflation) for transfers to persons below their children's generation.

Through the use of a charitable lead unitrust, you can pass more than the allowed exemption to grandchildren free of this tax.

Example: Margaret transfers $3,000,000 to a charitable lead unitrust with an 8% payout. After 15 years the remaining property will be distributed to her grandchildren. She allocates her $1,030,000 exemption (for 2000) to the trust. No generation-skipping tax will apply. She will have leveraged her exemption from $1,030,000 to $3,000,000.

The charitable lead annuity trust doesn't work as well when grandchildren are beneficiaries. The amount of generation-skipping tax assessed at the termination of the trust depends on the worth of the property then, which cannot be determined in advance. Thus, it is generally more prudent to use a *unitrust* when grandchildren are beneficiaries.

Note: The percentages in the following charts are based on a representative discount rate and assume that a charity receives annual payments at the end of the year. We would be pleased to provide you or your advisor with the current deductible amount:

Transfer—Tax Deduction Percentages Allowed for Unitrusts					
Pay-out Rate	5 Years	10 Years	15 Years	20 Years	25 Years
5%	21.46	38.32	51.56	61.95	70.12
6%	25.27	44.16	58.27	68.82	76.70
7%	28.94	49.50	64.11	74.50	81.88
8%	32.45	54.38	69.18	79.18	85.94
9%	35.83	58.82	73.58	83.04	89.12
10%	39.07	62.88	77.38	86.22	91.60
11%	42.18	66.57	80.67	88.82	93.54
12%	45.16	69.92	83.51	90.95	95.04

Payout rate refers to the percentage of the value of trust property as determined annually. If $1,000,000 was transferred and a 7% payout selected, charity would receive each year % of that year's trust value. The amount would vary from year to year. As with the charitable lead annuity trust, the deduction is determined by matching payout rate and length of trust term.

Transfer—Tax Deduction Percentages Allowed for Annuity Trusts					
Pay-out Rate	5 Years	10 Years	15 Years	20 Years	25 Years
5%	21.06	36.80	48.56	57.35	63.92
6%	25.27	44.16	58.27	68.82	76.70
7%	29.49	51.52	67.99	80.29	89.48
8%	33.70	58.88	77.70	91.76	100.00
9%	37.91	66.24	87.41	100.00	100.00
10%	42.12	73.60	97.12	100.00	100.00
11%	46.34	80.96	100.00	100.00	100.00
12%	50.55	88.32	100.00	100.00	100.00

Payout rate refers to the percentage of the initial value of the property transferred to the trust. If $1,000,000 was transferred and a 7% payout selected, charity would receive $70,000 each year. For a 15-year trust, 67.99% ($679,860) would be deductible for gift and estate taxes

Why does this benefit a charity in a meaningful way?

Most charities are in need of funding right now. If the immediate needs are not being met, then the Charitable Lead Trust is the best gifting strategy because income to the organization must begin immediately. An outright gift or donation is always preferred, yet the Lead Trust equates to a reliable source of income that is ongoing. It should be expressed that if charities concentrated on gifts from Lead Trusts, then their budget would be more predictable than with other fundraising activities. For example, ten well-heeled estates each donating $1,000,000 to a Charitable

Lead Trust at 8% pay-out would give a charity $800,000 a year. If this is reloaded each year, it would be an excellent way to sustain a charity.

THE CHARITABLE REMAINDER TRUST

A Charitable Remainder Trust can accomplish several purposes. While the trust-principal eventually goes to charity, its use can result in considerable savings in income, gift, and estate taxes.

The Charitable Remainder Trust (CRT) is an effective technique not only for giving but also for providing a mechanism for the transfer of property from one generation to the next without incurring any gift or estate tax liability. The grantor of the CRT may also continue to receive payments from the trust after the property is transferred to the trust for a designated period, or for a term covering an individual's lifetime, either the grantor's lifetime or that of the grantor and any other designated individuals.

The principal drawback of establishing a CRT is that the grantor gives up control of the property. The grantor has virtually no right to alter the provisions of the trust or to determine the fate of the property transferred to the trust.

The most effective use of the CRT is to transfer highly appreciated long-term-capital-gain property to it, since the trust will not be subject to income tax on the capital gain if the property is sold. In addition to avoiding gift and estate taxes on the property transferred to the trust, no income tax is incurred on the appreciation of the property in the hands of the donor or after it is transferred to the trust. Additionally, these tax avoidance techniques may be accomplished without decreasing the amount of property eventually left to the heirs of the grantor of the CRT.

Advantages and Disadvantages

The principal advantages of a CRT are as follows:

- An income tax charitable deduction in the year in which the trust is funded.
- Avoidance of capital gains tax on the sale of appreciated property after it is transferred to the trust.
- No gift or estate tax is incurred on the value of the property either when the property is transferred to the trust or on the death of the grantor.
- An income interest is retained and the grantor and others may receive periodic payments for the duration of the trust.

How the CRT Works

An individual creates a trust for the benefit of a charity, which is an organization qualified under IRC Sec. 501(c)(3). There is no estate or gift tax liability incurred when the trust is created and the grantor transfers property to the trust. The grantor retains an income interest in the trust and may continue to receive payments from the trust for a specified term of not more than twenty years or for the grantor's lifetime and the lifetimes of any successor beneficiaries designated in the original trust agreement. A charitable deduction for income tax purposes is allowed to the grantor for the present value of the remainder interest in the trust when the CRT is funded. The trust is not subject to tax on its income. However, the non-charitable beneficiaries will be subject to income tax on any money or property distributed to them. When the last surviving income beneficiary dies or the trust term expires, the property is transferred to the charity pursuant to the terms of the trust.

Types of CRTs

There are two types of CRTs: the Charitable Remainder Annuity Trust (CRAT) and the Charitable Remainder Unitrust (CRUT). Depending on the individual's needs and goals, either type of CRT might be appropriate.

A CRAT provides for payments of a fixed amount to the non-charitable beneficiary at least annually during the trust term. The annual fixed payment amount may not be less than five percent of the initial fair market value of the trust principal.

A CRUT results in payments to the non-charitable income beneficiary at a fixed percentage of the annual fair market value of the trust property not lower than five percent. The trust property, therefore, must be revalued at the beginning of each year in which the trust is in existence to determine the amount of the payment to which the non-charitable beneficiary is entitled.

The CRAT provides for a fixed payment. The grantor will always know what the income from the trust will be regardless of what the trust income actually is or of any changes in the value of the trust principal. The CRUT provides for a payment based on the value of the trust property and may increase or decrease from year to year.

Once the CRAT is created and funded, no additional contributions may be made to the trust by the grantor. However, in a CRUT, additional contributions to the trust may be made if provided for in the trust agreement.

Factors to consider: Whether a grantor should choose a unitrust or an annuity trust is a decision that should be arrived at after careful consideration of all the factors involved and evaluation of the grantor's goals by the grantor and financial advisor.

The CRAT does not provide for any protection against inflation during the term of the trust, since the payment is fixed in the initial year and does not change. However, there is no market risk assumed by the non-charitable CRAT beneficiary, either. If the value of the trust property declines, the non-charitable beneficiary still receives the full annuity. The charitable remainder beneficiary assumes the market risk. On the other hand, the CRUT provides some measure of protection against inflation risk during the term of the trust, provided the value of the trust property increases at the rate of inflation. The non-charitable beneficiary does, however, assume some measure of market risk under a CRUT scenario, since the annual payments are based upon an annual valuation of the trust property and any decline in the value of the trust property, temporary or otherwise, will result in a decrease in the unitrust payments. Generally, the longer the expected term of the trust, based on the life expectancies of the non-charitable beneficiaries, the greater the advantages of the unitrust due to the ongoing inflation risk associated with the CRAT. However, a conservative client may wish to ignore such risk for the guarantee of a fixed payment amount. Also, if hard-to-value property, such as real estate, artwork, or non-publicly traded securities, is used to fund the trust, or will be held by the trust during its term, the CRAT might be preferable to the CRUT since the property held in the CRUT must be revalued each year.

Charitable Remainder Trusts

THE CANDIDATES
- **Donors/Benefactors of a Charity**—looking to leave large sums of money to the Charity, while not giving up control.

- **Individuals**—with highly appreciated assets (typical CRTs have assets with $1,000,000 or more, but some have been done with $50,000 or more).
- **Business Owners**—wanting to use the CRT as an alternative to, or in addition to, a pension. The CRT isn't subject to ERISA or other taxes, or to any contribution limits.

THE BENEFACTORS OF CHARITABLE REMAINDER TRUSTS

- **Private Colleges and Universities** have traditionally been the leading benefactors of Charitable Gift Annuities through strong marketing campaigns and funding drives.
- **Hospitals and Public Universities** – have begun to increase marketing efforts, and are anticipated to increase market shares in the coming years.

THE CHARITABLE GIFT ANNUITY

Charitable Gift / Guaranteed Income for Life

Would you like to give to your passion and receive income for life? (Is that a trick question?)

Annuity comes from the word "annuitization" which means, "to pay out on a regular schedule." The Charitable Gift Annuity does just that. It pays you income for your life remainder and the life of your spouse or children if you choose. You begin by giving a tax-deductible donation to a charity, and that charity pays out income. Income can be deferred to start at a later date, or at retirement years. However, a great many of our clients have chosen to begin their monthly income right away.

The Charitable Gift Annuity (CGA) is a 130-year-old technique that has helped millions in charitable causes and would be described as a true win-win situation for both donor and charity.

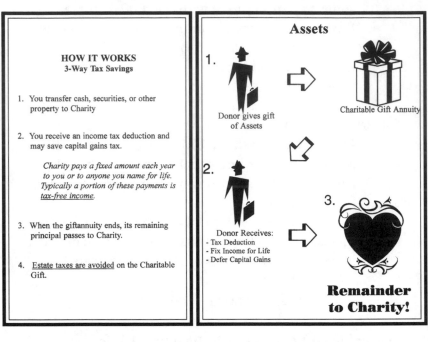

HOW IT WORKS
3-Way Tax Savings

1. You transfer cash, securities, or other property to Charity

2. You receive an income tax deduction and may save capital gains tax.

   Charity pays a fixed amount each year to you or to anyone you name for life. Typically a portion of these payments is tax-free income.

3. When the giftannuity ends, its remaining principal passes to Charity.

4. Estate taxes are avoided on the Charitable Gift.

Assets

1. Donor gives gift of Assets

Charitable Gift Annuity

2. Donor Receives:
- Tax Deduction
- Fix Income for Life
- Defer Capital Gains

3.

Remainder to Charity!

The CGA is *similar* to the Charitable Remainder Trust. It provides the following investor benefits:
- Direct your own contribution.
- Provide an income tax deduction.
- Reduce Estate tax.
- Delay substantial capital gain or ordinary income tax on appreciated assets.
- Provide income for Life and Asset Protection.
- Allow a portion of CGA distributions to be deemed return of principal, which reduces taxable income.

THESE ARE THE RULES
    a. The donation is irrevocable.
    b. The donation can have no conditions attached.

c. You can't change the payout once it has been established.
d. At death, the remainder interest goes to a charity.
e. Your surviving family members can direct "gifted"
monies through a Family Foundation or a Donor
Advised Account at the event of death if the annuity account is established toward that disbursement.

THESE ARE THE BENEFITS
a. You can donate numerous different assets such as
stocks, bonds, real estate, businesses, and mutual
funds.
b. You take an immediate tax deduction and may carry
the balance forward for 5 years (or until it's used
up, whichever comes first).
c. You can reduce capital gain or ordinary income taxes
on appreciated assets through the Charitable Gift
Annuity (CGA).
d. The Charitable Gift Annuity provides a steady stream
of income for life, a portion of which is non-tax-
able.
e. You avoid estate taxes on the CGA and income from
the CGA can be used to fund additional purchases
of life insurance to benefit family members.

SUMMARY OF BENEFITS /
ONE MILLION DOLLAR ASSET

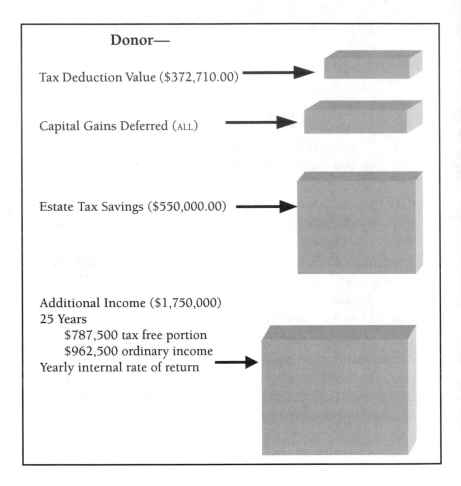

Donor—

Tax Deduction Value ($372,710.00)

Capital Gains Deferred (ALL)

Estate Tax Savings ($550,000.00)

Additional Income ($1,750,000)
25 Years
    $787,500 tax free portion
    $962,500 ordinary income
Yearly internal rate of return

COMBINE THE CHARITABLE GIFT ANNUITY OR
CHARITABLE REMAINDER TRUST WITH
A FOUNDATION FOR YOUR FAMILY

Why Would an Investor Create a Foundation and a Charitable Gift Annuity?

1. Establishing a foundation or Donor Advised Account, will give the donor an immediate income tax deduction up front, or can be spread over six (6) years.
2. Establishing a Charitable Gift Annuity will give the Donor income for life, which they can control, defer or take immediately.
3. Donor can eliminate some gains on appreciated assets.
4. Donor reduces estate taxes and can leave the assets to their own family foundations.
5. Donor will have more money after taxes for self, family, and Family Foundation.

CHARITABLE GIFT ANNUITY AND A DONOR ADVISED "FAMILY FOUNDATION"

Donor	C.G.A	Donor Income
Exchanges assets for CGA Receives Deduction Partial by-pass of Capital Gains Tax favorable Income Stream	Charitable Gift Annuity invests from sale of assets, pays a fixed percent income to original donor. (Monthly, Quarterly, Bi-Annual or Annual pay-out)	Receives fixed pay-out for life—immediate or deferred at a higher pay-out.

Final Beneficiaries
The donor's own Family Foundation can be the recipient of the final gift. This will leave funds available for charitable purposes, and can be directed by donor's spouse or children.

☙ Chapter Seven ☞

WHERE IS ROBIN HOOD?
Or, Who's in Charge, Anyway?

The quest for the truth about Robin Hood remains in ballads and myths, as well as real accounts regarding outlaws and individuals who inspire people to question financial authorities. The legends and accounts of a Robin Hood character actually date back to the Normans in the 1070's.

Today Robin Hood is celebrated as a cunning, crafty philanthropist with a passion for people in need. His ability to outfox the Sheriff of Nottingham (the tax collector at that time) was legendary. To report that it was Robin Hood who said, "I rob from the rich and give to the poor," was not accurate. The legendary Robin Hood took money back from the tax collector to help the people of his day.

Robin Hood is probably a combination of real or imaginary people who used the alias "Robin Hood," as the famed British author, J.C. Holt concludes, "The answer then to the question, 'Who was Robin Hood?' must be . . . there were more than one."

In the real world, the new Robin Hood can be found with your financial advisors. Most CPAs, attorneys, and financial planners have more than adequate access to Advanced Charitable Gifting techniques. I've been involved in training financial advisors for many years. The problem with their advice to date may be that they are not in their specialty and focus. However, with new tax legislation pending and other trends in the industry, I predict a substantial effort will be launched soon by all the major financial supermarkets, banks, brokerages, insurance companies, CPA firms, et cetera. Heck, there is even a foundation called The Robin Hood Foundation!

LEAD, FOLLOW, OR GET OUT OF THE WAY!

Where is Robin Hood?
    Who should be in charge of the process? This is a story about four people named Everybody, Somebody, Anybody and Nobody. There was an important job to be done and Everybody was sure that Somebody would do it. Anybody could have done it, but Nobody did it. Somebody was angry about that, because it was Everybody's job. Everybody thought Anybody could do it, but Nobody realized that Everybody wouldn't do it. It ended up that Everybody blamed Somebody when Nobody did what Anybody could have.

    The story above illustrates that someone must lead the way. All of the four listed candidates must choose a leader. The leader of the team then keeps the other members informed. The process of safeguarding a family's financial capital and social capital is complicated and takes degrees of talent. It is recommended that these professionals be selected with due diligence and their reputation are verified.

The Attorney. The attorney is vital in the process, especially when the number of assets are diversified or there are complex transactions that need to be addressed. Even a simple will and trust can go wrong if the documents are not in order or according to state laws. Many trusts that have been drafted are not going to stand the test of time. In addition, a good attorney relationship to facilitate giving reviews and updates is also recommended.

The Accountant. This is the person who would be best suited to give exact financial figures. Tax liabilities or upcoming distribution of income, company profits, and so on, can really factor into an estate plan. Don't try this without a CPA. It is crucial to be exact and to not guess. Estate evaluation, business evaluation, wealth accumulation, all can be important factors that must be assessed.

The Financial Advisor. This person, if he or she has training and experience with the entire process, can be invaluable. In understanding the mindset of a financial advisor, one must remember the goal they seek to achieve. Grow your assets, preserve your assets, save on taxes. This is about as good as it gets. A good financial advisor can and does create ways to do this. This is how most of them really earn their commissions or fees and grow their referral business.

The Insurance Case Specialist. Is this a science or an art? Perseverance is a key word that comes to mind. Getting insurance really working for you or your heirs can be a challenge. In most cases, insurance will always work, but not all policies are created equal. Some underwriters can also really step up the dollars of protection.

This team can make a big difference in how much you and your family will be able to help with charitable causes. Remember, if you do not plan, the federal government or state government will be the chosen charity. In order to

expand or to insure your social capital will go to your selected charitable causes, you must go through the legal steps and planning steps.

Why do we need Estate Planning? Estate Planning is about death and taxes . . . two things that modern science has not been able to prevent thus far. The other significant part regarding Estate Planning is . . . who gets what—when—where—and how much? It goes without saying that most folks don't really have an absolute grasp of Estate Planning strategies and techniques. The absolute of who needs Estate Planning the most really lies in not who gains the most, but who stands to lose the most? It is a fact that death and taxes are designed to wreak havoc on the tranquility of the family unit. But even people without families can be in a position to lose when death and taxes hit.

Who needs Estate Planning the most? Anyone who is interested in transferring assets or has surviving family members needs Estate Planning. It is a misconception that only rich people need estate planning. The following sections on wills and probate, methods of holding title and the establishment of trusts as titleholder are crucial.

Wills & Probate

Traditionally, the most common method of passing title to heirs has been through the will. A will is a testamentary instrument which acts as a directive to the Probate Court, a special court established to supervise the administration of the estates of deceased individuals. This section summarizes the basic rules associated with the Probate process.

Here we will also briefly discuss some of the disadvantages inherent in the Probate system.

A. What is a Will?

A will is a written directive executed by a Testator (male) or Testatrix (female), designed to instruct the Probate Court as to how the decedent's estate should be distributed. A will does not hold or transfer title to anything. It merely directs the court as to how the estate should be distributed. Only the court has the power to actually transfer the assets to the heirs.

There are two types of wills, and both are equally valid and admissible in the Probate Court. The first type of will is a Statutory Will. This is a typed document that is signed at the end by the Testator or Testatrix. Two or three disinterested witnesses must also witness a Statutory Will. The number of required witnesses varies according to state law. California requires at least two disinterested witnesses.

The term "disinterested" means simply that the witness can under no circumstances be deemed to be capable of obtaining a beneficial interest in the will or the estate. Therefore, a disinterested witness may not be a beneficiary or even a remotely contingent beneficiary.

The second type of will is a Holographic Will. A Holographic Will must be written in the handwriting of the Testator, and it must be signed and dated in the handwriting of the Testator. A Holographic Will does not require any witnesses to be present. Perhaps one of the most famous Holographic Wills was the will allegedly handwritten by Howard Hughes, whereby Howard Hughes purportedly gave his entire estate to Melvin Dumar. The Nevada Probate Court, however, failed to accept this will as a valid testamentary instrument.

Wills are primarily contested on two grounds: lack of capacity and undue influence. If the Testator or Testatrix has not yet attained the age of majority or lacks the mental ability to comprehend the testamentary impact of his or her actions, then the will may be invalidated. If the Testator or Testatrix has been subject to some sort of severe undue influence, which caused the Testator or Testatrix to take actions he or she normally would not have taken, then the will may be invalidated by the court or by contesting beneficiaries subject to court approval.

B. The Duties of the Probate Court

When the Testator or Testatrix dies, the intervention of the Probate Court is necessary to prove the validity of the will, to appraise the value of the estate, to settle all of the debts and liabilities of the estate, and to ascertain the identity of the heirs and beneficiaries. Once the court has completed these tasks it is able to transfer title to the heirs.

The personal representative or executor is the individual appointed by the Testator to represent the Testator's estate in court. The probate referee is the court appointed individual who acts as the intermediary between the court and the personal representative while most of the more tedious accounting and business matters are being taken care of. In most cases, an attorney will also represent the personal representative in his efforts to negotiate the labyrinth of court filings and appearances. In many cases, accountants and real estate or stockbrokers will also be employed by the court or by the personal representative to assist in the estate settlement process.

C. What Types of Estates Go through Probate?

All estates that are being transferred by will must go through probate. There are basically two types of probate.

One is a summary probate and the other is a full statutory probate.

If the gross value of the entire estate falls under $100,000, a summary probate, which is an abbreviated form of the more lengthy statutory process, is all that is required. However, if the gross value of the real estate alone is greater than $20,000, then a probate for that real estate will still be required. When the gross value of the entire estate, including all real and personal property, is equal to or surpasses $100,000, then the entire estate must go through a complete statutory probate (California Probate Code '13100).

1. THE PURPOSE OF PROBATE

The real purpose of the Probate Court is to insure that an objective judicial body, trained in the administration of such matters, will be responsible for the evaluation of the will and the administration of the estate. It is theoretically better for a trained professional to handle such affairs rather than a lay person. With the objective Probate Court standing by, it is more difficult for fraud or circumvention contrary to the Testator's wishes to occur.

2. THE DISADVANTAGES OF PROBATE

Despite the good intentions of the legal system, there are many fundamental disadvantages associated with the probate process. Because of the tremendous number of forms, filings, and court appearances necessary to complete a probate in many states, the process is entirely too lengthy. In California, for example, the average probate requires 20 months before the court is free to transfer title of the remaining assets to the heirs. The expense of probate is also a problem. Combined, all the expenses incurred by the attorneys, the accountants, the executor, the court, the appraisers, and the probate referee may add up to over 8% of the estate's gross value!

It should be noted that without proper estate planning, many of the forms of holding title eventually end up in probate.

All community property must go through probate because there is no right of survivorship. Quasi-community property is also subject to probate. Separate property also goes through probate when no beneficiary has been designated. Any interest owned by a deceased Tenant in Common must go through probate, as well. And even where Joint Tenants might have owned property, at the death of the final Joint Tenant the property must still be transferred through the probate process if the surviving Joint Tenant failed to add subsequent Joint Tenants as successors in interest.

METHODS OF HOLDING TITLE

Title is the key to estate planning. The way a client holds title to an asset will determine the taxes, the liability exposure and the ultimate disposition of the asset. Many different methods of holding title have unique advantages. Very often the client has overlooked the disadvantages of a particular method of holding title in favor of the advantages. Sometimes a client has never been adequately informed as to all of the advantages and disadvantages as they relate to each method of holding title. The estate planner should be prepared to illustrate all of the ramifications of each form of title that the client is currently employing to hold assets, whether it is Joint Tenancy, Community Property, Quasi-Community Property, Separate Property, or Tenants in Common.

A. Joint Tenancy

When it comes to owning a home, most clients are joint tenants. Joint Tenancy is a form of undivided ownership, where each Joint Tenant owns an equal, undivided and yet separate interest in land. Joint Tenants share an equal and undivided interest in time, title, interest and possession as it relates to the land.

Joint Tenants also enjoy a right of survivorship whereby the deceased Joint Tenant passes all of his or her interest in the land to the surviving Joint Tenant(s) by operation of law, and without probate. When the final Joint Tenant dies, however, the property will be probated.

DISADVANTAGES OF JOINT TENANCY

While Joint Tenants enjoy the right of survivorship, often the right of survivorship can lead to unexpected and undesired results when the wrong person inherits an entire property simply because they survived the other Joint Tenants.

Unfortunately, Joint Tenants also have a diluted form of ownership and control, for no single Joint Tenant can sell or encumber the entire property without the consent of all other Joint Tenants.

Another disadvantage created by Joint Tenancy is liability exposure. A liability incurred by any single Joint Tenant may create a claim on the entire property, including the interests held by all over Joint Tenants. Some parents place children on title as Joint Tenants for convenience and because they have heard that if they do, the property will pass to the children without any probate. While this is true, the client should understand that the property is exposed to all of the debts intentionally or unintentionally incurred by any of the children.

Finally, Joint Tenants are hit especially hard by the Capital Gains Tax because Joint Tenancy results in a division of the Capital Gains Tax basis. Tax Basis on any property is the amount that was originally paid for the property, plus improvements, less depreciation. Tax Basis is basically tax free, and, if the property is ever sold, the client does not have to pay tax on the original basis. Many clients have a great amount of appreciation over and above the property's original basis. Again, the basis is basically equivalent to what the client paid for the land when the property was acquired. Unfortunately, only the pro rata portion tax basis owned by each Joint Tenant can be stepped up at the death of that Joint Tenant. The tax-free basis held by the surviving Joint Tenants remains constant until their own death. The problem occurs when the surviving Joint Tenants want to sell the property. If the surviving Joint Tenants sell the land, they must pay a Capital Gains Tax on their share of the appreciated taxable gain. This is perhaps the most significant disadvantage associated with Joint Tenancy.

B. Tenants in Common

Tenants in Common differ from Joint Tenants in that the interests of each Tenant in Common need not be equal and there is no right of survivorship. If one Tenant in Common dies, instead of passing to the surviving Tenants in Common as is the case with Joint Tenancy, the deceased Tenant in Common's individual interest in the land may pass by a testamentary device to their chosen beneficiaries after going through probate.

C. Community Property

There are eight Community Property states in the United States, including Arizona, California, Idaho, Louisiana,

Nevada, New Mexico, Texas and Washington. In these states all property and earnings acquired after marriage belong one-half to the Husband and one-half to the Wife. Community Property, then, is all property acquired after marriage, and it belongs equally to each spouse. The only exception to this rule is Separate Property, which under certain circumstances defined below, belongs solely to the Spouse to whom it was given. When a married couple divorces, the court usually gives the Husband half of the value in the estate and the Wife half of the value in the estate. This is because most married couples in California and other Community Property states primarily own property that was obtained during marriage and is owned equally by each spouse.

Unlike Joint Tenancy, Community Property has no right of survivorship. When one spouse dies owning Community Property, the Community Property does not automatically pass to a surviving spouse. Rather, Community Property must be probated. In fact, when one spouse dies, that deceased spouse is free under Community Property law to leave that fifty percent Community Property interest to any other person and not necessarily to a surviving spouse. So, even though Community Property may be transferred at death to any person, spouse or non-spouse, the fact that this transfer must occur through the probate court is generally the biggest problem associated with Community Property.

D. Quasi-Community Property

Quasi-Community Property is property whose site is in a non-Community Property State and was acquired by a married couple who reside in a Community Property state, such as California, in which the property would have been considered Community Property had the couple acquired it while living in a Community Property state. Quasi-Community Property is treated for legal purposes just like Community Property.

E. Separate Property

Separate Property is property that an individual owned before he or she was married, or property that was given to or inherited by a person after they were married. A spouse has no claim on another spouse's Separate Property. Additionally, the earnings from Separate Property are also considered Separate Property, just as the earnings, dividends and income from Community Property are considered to be Community Property.

F. The Totten Trust

When an individual opens a bank account or titles a stock or investment in his or her name, in Trust for or as Trustee for someone else, a Totten Trust has been created. At the death of the original account holder, the beneficiary need only present a death certificate to receive the proceeds.

THE TRUST AS A METHOD OF HOLDING TITLE

A Trust is simply another way of holding legal title, similar to Community Property and to Joint Tenancy, but with its own set of advantages. A Trust is slightly more complicated than most methods of holding title, however, because there are two forms of title: legal title and beneficial title. The Trustees of the Trust hold Legal Title and the Beneficial Title is owned by the Beneficiaries of the Trust. Trusts have certain requirements and attributes that differentiate them from other methods of holding title.

A. General Requirements

Like Criminal Law, Securities Law or Constitutional Law, the body of Trust Law, long established as part of our Common Law, contains certain necessary elements.

1. TRUSTOR

Each Trust, by law, must have a Trustor. The Trustor is the Creator or Testator of the Trust who signs the Trust into existence.

2. TRUSTEE

Every Trust must have a Trustee responsible for administering the Trust assets for the benefit to the beneficiaries of the Trust. Trust Law allows more than one Trustee at a time. When a Husband and Wife, as Trustors, create a Trust, they typically name themselves as Co-Trustees, together, with equal authority. And, quite often, the Trustors will designate that at their demise their children will act together as Co-Trustees to administer assets for the benefit of the beneficiaries.

The Restatement of Trusts dictates that the Trustee comply with the Prudent Man Rule. The Prudent Man Rule requires that the Trustee administer all trust assets in a very prudent, conservative manner, just as a prudent man would administer his own assets. Speculative investments and activities are prohibited, and should the Trust experience any loss because of speculative investments, the Trustee is personally liable for the loss.

3. BENEFICIARIES

Every Trust must also have at least one beneficiary. It may also have many beneficiaries. For most married couples who create a Living Revocable Trust, the couple will name themselves as the initial beneficiaries, entitled to use and enjoy all of the assets of the trust until the death of the second spouse. At the death of the surviving spouse, only then will the final beneficiaries' rights vest.

4. CAPACITY

This element of the Trust Law requires that the Trustors have the mental capacity to understand the testamentary import of their actions at the time of the creation of the trust. They must be able to comprehend the significance of their actions. They must also be of legal age. This varies from state to state, but is 18 in the State of California.

5. LEGAL INTENT

The Trustors must have legal intent to create a Trust and the administrative provisions contained in the trust must obligate the Trustee to carry out actions that are legal in all respects.

6. CORPUS

Importantly, a Trust must have corpus, or assets, at the time of the creation of the trust. Without assets the law does not allow a trust to exist. Consequently, when a trust finally distributes its assets to the ultimate heirs and beneficiaries, it then lacks corpus, contains no assets, and ceases to exist.

B. General Attributes

Trusts are popular because of their many distinctive attributes. Perhaps the most important attributes of the Trust are its ability to maintain privacy, its ability to be revoked or amended, its ability to avoid probate entirely, and its ability to diminish certain taxes.

1. A Trust Maintains Privacy

Unlike Wills, which become publicly recorded documents, Trusts are completely private. The Trustor(s) must sign all Trusts, and most Trusts are also signed by a notary public, which acknowledges the signatures of the Trustors. At all times during Trust administration, during and after the lives of the Trustors, the privacy of the contents and terms of the Trust may be maintained. A Trust is not a publicly recorded document and does not go through the public probate process. Rather, one purpose of the Trust is to insure private administration without public court scrutiny or participation.

2. A Trust Is Revocable

While there are two families of Trusts, Revocable and Irrevocable, one primary advantage of the Revocable Trust is that it can be terminated or revoked in its entirety at any time after its creation. Irrevocable Trusts, of course, cannot be revoked or terminated after they are signed.

3. A Trust Can Be Amended

Revocable Trusts can be amended to accommodate any changing circumstances. The Revocable Trust can be amended at any time after its creation by the execution of a simple amendment signed by both of the Creators (Trustors) of the Trust. Some types of trusts become partially Irrevocable at the death of the first spouse, but any living Trustor is usually free to make alterations over all portions of the Trust that they control.

4. A Trust Does Not Go Through Probate

The Trust is a form of ongoing title. Once the initial Trustee dies, a successor Trustee automatically succeeds to the legal title ownership of all Trust assets. This transfer of ownership occurs automatically, by operation of law, without the intervention of the probate court. Once the successor Trustee comes into control, he or she is free to administer assets for the benefit of the final beneficiaries, as the Trust documents indicate.

5. The Rule Against Perpetuities

Clients will occasionally ask whether it is possible to create a trust that will last forever, one that will never terminate. Under our current law, this is no longer possible because of the Rule Against Perpetuities. The Rule Against Perpetuities limits the lifetime of a trust to a specific period. According to the Rule, a trust can only exist for the lifetime of the youngest living being alive at the time of the creation of the trust, and then twenty-one years beyond.

6. Additional Requirements

Although a Trust is designed to avoid probate, because it is a testamentary instrument, it is still subject to many of the same requirements that a will is. A Trust cannot be the result of any undue influence. One should take care to observe the condition, mindset, and surroundings of the client as the client creates the Trust, making sure that there are no family members or friends who are exerting pressure on or manipulating the client in any way.

The Trustor must also have the capacities of age and of mental understanding in order to create a Trust. The Associate must work with very elderly or ill clients in an extremely careful manner to make sure that the client hears, understands, and approves of what is being said and done. Otherwise, the Trust could be contested and invalidated in the probate court.

Types of Trusts

Different types of Trusts can be created to meet the specific needs of any given client. While some Trusts are quite simple, others are more complex and can be designed to secure a wide range of control and tax advantages. Becoming familiar with the different types of Trusts is vitally important to becoming an effective Estate Planner.

Two Types of Trusts: Revocable & Irrevocable

There are basically two families of Trusts: Revocable and Irrevocable. Revocable Trusts are the most common type of trust. They can be revoked or amended any time after their creation. Irrevocable Trusts, on the other hand, cannot be revoked or amended in any way after their creation.

Following is a list and a general description of the Revocable and Irrevocable Trusts most commonly used today.

A. Revocable Trusts

Revocable Trusts can be altered, amended or terminated entirely at any time during the Trustor's lifetime. Revocable Trusts are commonly referred to as Living Trusts or Family Trusts. Revocable Trusts are all basically "Inter Vivos" Trusts, which must be created while the Trustor is alive. The most commonly employed Revocable Trusts are listed below.

1. The Single Trust

An unmarried individual creates the Single Trust. It is designed to hold the individual's assets until his or her death, and at death will operate to transfer the assets to the Trustor's chosen beneficiaries.

2. THE MARRIED SEPARATE TRUST

The Married Separate Trust is also a Single Trust, but for a married person. It is typically used in those rare occasions where the Community Property of a marital estate is going to be eliminated and converted into Separate Property for asset protection or organization purposes and held by a separate Husband's Trust and a separate Wife's Trust.

3. THE RESULTING MARRIED TRUST

This Trust is designed for married couples whose net estate value does not exceed the maximum applicable federal estate tax exclusion, currently $675,000. The Resulting Married Trust is a simple trust that passes all assets from the first deceased spouse to the surviving spouse. At the death of the surviving spouse, all remaining assets are transferred to the final heirs and beneficiaries according to the special distribution terms of the trust.

4. THE A/B TRUST

The A/B Trust is a special trust for married couples. The A/B Trust does two things that a simple Resulting Trust does not do. It allows a married couple to ultimately pass $1,350,000 to their heirs instead of a mere $675,000, and it also protects the deceased spouse's heirs from being disinherited or revoked by the surviving spouse.

At the death of the first spouse, the A/B Trust divides into two shares, an A Share, commonly referred to as the Survivor's Share, and a B Share, commonly referred to as the Decedent's Share. One-half of the estate, up to $675,000, or up to the equivalent of the maximum individual federal estate and gift tax exemption, can be placed into the B Trust. All of the balance in the estate passes to the survivor, into the A Trust.

At the creation of the trust, the couple can elect to give the surviving spouse certain rights over the B Trust at the death of the first spouse. The three rights that a surviving spouse may have over the B Trust (the Decedent's Trust) are as follows: The surviving spouse may receive all of the income from the B Trust, the surviving spouse may use 5% of the principal of the B Trust or $5,000 per year from the principal of the B Trust, whichever is greater, and/or the surviving spouse may invade and use all 100% of the principal of the B Trust if it is necessary for the health, education, maintenance, or welfare of the surviving spouse, or if it is necessary to help the surviving spouse remain in the living standard to which they had become accustomed at the time of the first spouse's death.

This division of the A/B Trust, which occurs at the first death, occurs primarily for tax reasons. However, there is one added benefit: the Decedent's Trust, (the B Trust), is Irrevocable. Even though the surviving spouse can utilize the assets of the B Trust, the surviving spouse cannot revoke, alter, or amend the beneficiaries of the deceased spouse's B Trust, even if the surviving spouse remarries. Nevertheless, the surviving spouse is entitled to revoke or amend any portion of the A Trust, over which he or she is in complete control.

When this division into the A and B shares of the Family Trust takes place at the death of the first spouse, there is still no distribution to the ultimate beneficiaries. All the assets typically remain in the B Trust for the use of the surviving spouse. Only at the death of the surviving spouse are what remains of the A and B Trusts finally distributed to the ultimate heirs and beneficiaries.

5. THE QTIP TRUST (THE A/B/C TRUST)

The QTIP Trust is also known as and sometimes referred to as the ABC Trust. The QTIP Trust functions in much the same manner as the AB Trust, with one important exception. At the death of the first spouse, the Trust divides into three shares, the A, B and C shares.

As in the case of the AB Trust, all of the surviving spouse's community property and separate property flows into the surviving spouse's A Share. All of the deceased spouse's community and separate property flows into the B and C Shares. If the value of the deceased spouse's one-half interest in all of the estate's community property combined with his or her separate property exceeds the amount of the maximum individual federal estate and gift tax exemption, (currently $625,000), then all the excess of the deceased spouse's assets flows over into the third share of the trust known as the C Share of the Trust. The C Share is referred to as the QTIP Share. QTIP stands for **Q**ualified **T**erminable **I**nterest **P**roperty. The government requires that all of the income from the QTIP share must be paid to the surviving spouse during the remainder of the surviving spouse's lifetime. At the death of the surviving spouse, the income interest in the deceased spouse's QTIP Share will terminate. All three trusts will be subject to the federal estate and gift tax to the extent that they surpass the doubled federal estate and gift tax exemption, or $1,350,00 (I.R.C. '2523(f)). If the spouses so elect at the creation of the trust, the surviving spouse can obtain certain other benefits from the QTIP share for the health, education and welfare of the surviving spouse, at the hands of the independent trustee of the C Share, (QTIP Share).

One should note that the AB Trust and the ABC Trust (QTIP Trust) each protect the same amount of the estate from federal estate and gift taxes, $1,350,000. The only real difference between the two trusts is that with the QTIP Trust a deceased spouse can literally protect a full one-half of the estate from diminishment at the hands of a surviving spouse, rather than just $675,000, as is the case with the AB Trust.

Example: Mr. and Mrs. Jones' estate is valued at $3 million. At Mr. Jones death, one-half of the estate, $1.5 million, remains in the survivor's A Trust. The deceased spouse's assets also total $1.5 million. Accordingly, $675,000 is transferred into the B Trust to secure the deceased spouse's individual federal estate tax exemption. All of the excess of the deceased spouse's assets over and above $675,000 is transferred into the QTIP Share (C Share). Therefore, in this case $825,000 would be transferred into the QTIP Share. At the creation of the trust, the spouses decide what rights of invasion and use over the B and C Shares will be available to the surviving spouse. The survivor must receive at least all of the income from the QTIP Share or the unlimited marital deduction will be disallowed. Later, at the death of the surviving spouse, all three trusts can be combined and distributed to the heirs. The A and B Trusts will each be entitled to $675,000 in federal estate tax exemption, totaling $1,350,000 in available tax exemption. All of the excess, $1,650,000, will be subject to the federal estate and gift tax at the applicable tax rate.

6. THE QDOT TRUST

The QDOT Trust (Qualified Domestic Trust) is primarily for non-citizens. Under current tax law a non-citizen is not entitled to the unlimited marital deduction. To overcome this limitation, Congress allows the non-citizen to designate a Trustee to hold title to his assets at his death for the benefit of the surviving spouse. In this manner, the non-citizen can obtain the advantages of the unlimited marital deduction, just as a citizen can by creating a QTIP Trust.

B. Irrevocable Trusts

An Irrevocable Trust is used in special circumstances for larger estates or for certain highly appreciated assets. Irrevocable Trusts cannot be altered or amended by the Trustor after they have been created. There are many types of Irrevocable Trust. Perhaps the most popular are the Charitable Trusts discussed in this book.

TOP TEN REASONS WHY YOU NEED A LIVING TRUST WITH A CHARITABLE GIFTING TRUST:

1. Gives Peace of Mind
2. Avoids Probate
3. Eliminates Capital Gains Tax
4. Reduces or Eliminates the Federal Estate and Gift Tax
5. Preserves Privacy
6. Provides Incapacitation Clause
7. Has Tailored Distribution
8. Is Convenient, Revocable and Amendable
9. Provides Organization
10. Is Legal Nationwide

HOW ARE ESTATE TAXES PAID?

"There are two systems of taxation in this country, one
for the informed and one for the uninformed."
—The Honorable Judge Learned Hand

Estate and death taxes are due and payable in cash within
nine months after the taxpayer's death. This means after
the Death of the second spouse. Basically there are four
ways to pay this tax:

1. **The taxpayer may pay in cash.** In many cases the children have not accumulated enough money to satisfy the heavy amount. This event often results in liquidation of family heirlooms, valuable property, and even the sale of entire businesses.

2. **The taxpayer may borrow the money.** This only defers the problem and could make matters worse financially for the heirs. The money will still have to be repaid, with interest. This will include installment payments to the IRS.

3. **The executor may choose to liquidate assets.** If the market for these assets is soft, or weak, then these assets could be sold at a great loss to the heirs.

4. **The taxpayer may arrange to have these estate costs already prepaid by the purchase of life insurance.** As discussed in an earlier chapter, the insurance itself must be placed into an ILIT (Irrevocable Life Insurance Trust). This strategy is effective in paying this tax with discounted dollars. The proceeds will be paid outside of

the estate and thus be exempt from probate. The life insurance provides the needed cash in a predictable manner when it is needed.

Each taxpayer has a unified credit, which can be used to offset the first dollars, which would need to be paid to the government. By the year 2006, that credit will be one million dollars per taxpayer. Through use of the A/B Credit Shelter Trust, each spouse will be able to utilize two million combined, in the year 2006.

Are There Other Ways I Can Discount the Tax My Children Will Owe to Uncle Sam?

YES! But beware—you may become an imposter of charity! This means that other discounting strategies can be used to increase wealth and facilitate wealth transfer; however, they do not benefit charities in a meaningful way and are not used in a charitable gifting technique. I mention these strategies because they serve a major purpose if they save valuable dollars, which could be utilized "later on" towards charitable gifts.

WEALTH TRANSFER STRATEGIES:

1. Family Limited Partnerships

2. Income in Respect of Decedent

3. Private Annuities

4. Grantor Retained Income Trusts

5. Qualified Personal Residence Trusts

6. The Self-Canceling Installment Note

Family Limited Partnerships

FLPS: Family Limited Partnerships are utilized by the family members to make discounted gifts to other family members. This technique could result in significantly lower estate taxes and at the same time still allow control of the family assets and how they are managed.

All the partners of the FLP are family members. These partnerships have two classes of partners. The General partner takes care of the management and daily activity. The Limited Partners will not have managerial control in this case. Typically the parents will be the General Partner and the children, grandchildren, or a trust established in their name, the Limited Partners.

When the FLP is formed, the General Partner will transfer assets to the partnership. A family owned business or real estate is a good transaction for FLP assets. If only a minority interest in the asset is transferred, substantial valuation discounts can be warranted. Therefore, by transferring the minority interest in the asset, the overall value of the FLP is going to be less than the actual value of the asset transferred. This will then lower the value of the estate and the estate taxes that would be assessed. The discounts for the transfer of minority interest range from 15% to 30%. If the parents also gift units of limited partnership to the children and grandchildren, then an even greater discount is created.

The FLP can combine the two discounts (the minority interest discount and the non-marketability discount) and the family can obtain an overall combined discount as high as 60% percent or greater. Family limited partnerships must have a true business purpose in order to substantiate the discounts before the IRS. Therefore, only business assets such as a family business or commercial real estate property should be used to fund the trust. The discount must be adequately substantiated. These discounts are justified because the limited partners only have a minority interest which exercises no control (the limited partners have no management powers) and there is little or no market for the shares of the limited partnership interests.

Family Limited Partnerships have notable estate planning advantages:

1. The FLP can prohibit limited partners from encumbering their ownership interests.

2. The partnership can be amended and is not an irrevocable trust

3. The property can be protected in the event of divorce, because it is difficult to convert to community property.

4. The general partner maintains full control over the assets.

5. There is asset protection because the limited partners' shares are not attractive to a judgment creditor.

6. Gift and estate taxes should be lowered substantially because the valuation of the separate interests is discounted.

INCOME IN RESPECT OF DECEDENT

Items of Income in Respect of Decedent, or IRD, include assets in qualified retirement plans, U.S. savings bonds (untaxed interest), accounts receivable, variable or fixed annuities, renewal commissions of insurance agents, accrued royalties under a patent license, payments on installment obligations, and a deceased partner's share of partnership income. All are subject to both estate tax and income tax. A charitable bequest of IRD produces both an estate tax and an income tax deduction (IRS Tax Code 642(c) (1)). In making charitable gifts, it is highly recommended that assets that constitute Income in Respect of Decedent always be used.

One of the least understood aspects of commercial annuities (not to be confused with the Charitable Gift Annuity) is how they are taxed at the death of the Owner/Annuitant. If the Owner/Annuitant's beneficiary is a spouse, the spouse can continue the annuity with all the rights and privileges of the deceased Owner/Annuitant. Alternatively, if the owner/annuitant's beneficiary is a non-spouse, the non-spouse must distribute the annuity contract within five years or annuitize the contract for the period not greater than the beneficiary's life expectancy. If the beneficiary chooses to annuitize the contract, the annuity must begin within one year of the Owner/Annuitant's death.

Upon distribution of the annuity, whether in a lump sum or annuitized, it is commonly believed that the non-spouse beneficiary is required to pay ordinary income tax on the gain in the annuity. While technically true, most people fail to realize that the beneficiary receives an itemized deduction equal to the estate taxes paid by the Owner/Annuitant's estate on the gain in the annuity. This relief is provided under the Internal Revenue Code's Income in Respect of Decedent (IRD) rules. The effect of the IRD itemized deduction is to substantially reduce the amount of income tax due on the gain in the annuity.

Example: Assume that an Owner/Annuitant with a $3,000,000 taxable estate invested $200,000 in an annuity and it grew to $500,000. At his or her death the beneficiary, if they are in the 36% federal income tax bracket, would pay 17% federal income tax on the gain in the annuity.

Of course, each non-spouse beneficiary's effective federal income tax rate on the gain in the annuity will differ depending on the size of the owner's estate and the federal income tax bracket of the beneficiary.

CALCULATION FOR BENEFICIARY—INCOME TAX OWED

Taxable Income from Annuity	$300,000
Less Tax Deduction from IRD	-$159,000
Net Taxable Income from Annuity	$141,000
36% Federal Income Tax Bracket	X 36%
Tax Payable	$50,760
Effective Federal Income Tax Rate	**17%**
	($50,760 / $300,000)

The tax deduction from IRD is equal to the estate taxes paid by the original owner of the Annuity

It is also the case that the wealthier the client the less taxes are due on the buildup inside the annuity.

PRIVATE ANNUITIES

A private annuity is a contract between the annuitant and someone other than an insurance company. IRD rules will not apply. This private annuity is usually created when an older family member transfers assets to a younger family member who makes an unsecured promise to pay a lifetime annuity to the transferor. The goal of this technique is to reduce the estate owner's potential death tax liability by eliminating assets from the estate during his or her lifetime.

Additionally, nothing gets taxed in the annuitant's estate, because nothing remains to be paid after the annuitant's death. Unless at the time of the transfer the value of the annuity is less than the value of the property transferred, there will be no gift tax on the transaction. The value of the annuity is determined by reference to the annuity tables set by the Internal Revenue Code regulations. The tables can't be used if the donor is terminally ill or if there is a 50% chance of probability that the individual will die within one year.

Features and advantages of Private Annuities are:
1. When compared to a gift to a family member, the private annuity results in no gift tax.
2. The asset transferred will be kept out of the owner's estate
3. If the owner needs income during his or her lifetime, the annuity payments will be available.
4. A portion of the annuity payments will be excluded from the owner's taxable income.
5. The asset transferred will immediately receive a new income tax basis to the purchaser equal to the then present value of the annuity payments to be made. The owner, without using a private annuity, could not have made a sale of the underlying asset to third party without paying a capital gains tax, which would have reduced the after tax net proceeds.

GRANTOR RETAINED INCOME TRUSTS (GRITS)

Perhaps considered the "Granddaddy" of the discounting of assets to be transferred to Heirs, this technique is an irrevocable trust into which the grantor transfers assets designated, after a term of years, to the grantor's heirs. During the term of the trust years the grantor actually receives the trust income. The trust can be any number of years determined by the grantor. The longer the trust, the greater the present value of the grantor's retained interest. The present value of the grantor's retained income interest is subtracted from the value of the GRIT and therefore results in great savings in gift and estate tax.

The grantor's age, the value of the property transferred, and the term of years of the GRIT determine the valuation of the gift. Sizable estates holding property and other assets can be distributed to beneficiaries through GRIT on a discounted basis. This will dramatically lower the gift and estate taxes while freezing the value of the property transferred out of the estate of the grantor. Like the Charitable Remainder trust the GRIT has two payout schemes. The retained income interest of the grantor must be either an annuity amount or a unitrust amount. An annuity amount is structured as a fixed amount payable to the grantor each year, also referred to as a GRAT, Grantor Retained Annuity Trust. The unitrust amount is calculated as a fixed percentage of the transferred property payable to the grantor each year. This is sometimes referred to as the GRUT, Grantor Retained Unitrust, if the beneficiaries of the GRIT are not family members; you do not have to structure the income interest as a GRAT or a GRUT. If immediate family members are beneficiaries, then the retained income interest must be either an annuity amount or a unitrust amount.

Advantages of a Grantor Retained Income Trust (GRIT):

1. All gift taxes paid by the grantor are deductible from the grantor's estate.

2. The property in the GRIT is not taxed in the estate of the grantor at his or her death.
3. All appreciation on the subject property named in the GRIT avoids further gift taxes.
4. The grantor continues to receive income from the GRIT property for the entire term of the GRIT.
5. The property transferred to the GRIT is not taxed at its full value. It is only taxed to the extent that the value of the property exceeds the value of the grantor's retained interest.

QUALIFIED PERSONAL RESIDENCE TRUST (QPRT)

A QPRT is an irrevocable trust. The grantor transfers the personal residence to this trust. He or she retains the right to have exclusive use of the home for a chosen term of years. If the grantor survives the term of years of the trust, the residence is retained in further trust or is transferred in title to the trust beneficiaries. This concept is very much similar to the GRIT in that the value of the gift to the QPRT is discounted by subtracting the grantor's retained interest from the present value of the gift. The gift and estate taxes can therefore be greatly reduced, depending on the term of the trust. If the grantor wishes to, the personal residence can be leased from the beneficiaries after the trust terminates. This further reduces the taxable value of his or her estate while having frozen the value of the residence out of the estate at the discounted value.

People with large amounts of equity in their home or vacation home can use the QPRT and discount that equity out of their estate. If the Qualified Personal Residence Trust is properly drafted, there will be no income taxation on the grantor's use of the residence and the transfer of the property will not trigger a reassessment of the property taxes.

Also, as an alternative to leasing at fair market value, the grantor could purchase the property from GRIT near the end of the term. If the purchase is consummated prior to the expiration of the designated term period, it is possible to avoid income taxation on the sale.

THE SELF-CANCELLING INSTALLMENT NOTE (SCIN)

The Self-Cancelling Installment Note (SCIN) has many of the same advantages as the Private Annuity. The SCIN is a transaction whereby a person sells property to his or her family members on an installment basis. If the seller dies before the term of the note has expired; the balance of the amount due on the note will be cancelled. A self-cancelling installment note will not be included in the person's estate at death, if the note can reasonably be paid in full during the person's lifetime. The term of the note should be based on accepted mortality tables and should include an interest rate or purchase price premium because of possible early termination due to death.

It should also be noted, if the note itself is not paid in full at the time of death, that portion of the canceled note which represents unrealized capital gain on the sale will be included in your income for the year in which death occurred. This income tax liability can be deducted from your taxable estate.

THE FINAL WORD ON WEALTH TRANSFER TECHNIQUES

In conclusion, these techniques have similar objectives to the previously mentioned planned gifting ideas. The process in using these techniques creates retention by the donor of a term interest in the transferred asset. This is the very same retained interest which creates much of the tax advantages to planned giving. However, the Private Annuity, the Self Cancelling Installment note, the Qualified Personal Residence Trust, Family Limited Partnerships, and Grantor Retained Income Trusts, do not, I repeat, do not directly involve a charity in a direct way. These techniques do not assure anything to a charity. However, they are relevant because these techniques could compete against the planned giving aspects that this book believes to be highly desirable for the immediate family members and for building a legacy.

❧ *Chapter Eight* ☙

CASE STUDIES

CASE STUDY #1
MRS. SMITH

Mrs. Smith is a long-time church member. She is very dedicated in her faith, and wishes to give an outright gift. She wants to do this out of the goodness of her heart, and doesn't expect anything in return. The biggest question on her mind seems to be . . . how much can she give, and when should she give it?

Case Solution

Mrs. Smith may be best served by simply writing a check to the church—which she can do at any time, and in any amount. The donation is 100% deductible. The only limitation is that she can only deduct up to 50% of her adjusted gross income in any calendar year. If she has very little income, then she can carry the deduction forward for a five-year period, which may wipe out any income tax owed depending on the size of her gift. For example: If she gives a $1million gift, and her income is $50,000 per year, she can only deduct $25,000 per year against that income. That means that, multiplied by five years, she is able to deduct only $125,000 on a million-dollar gift. Basically, from a mathematical standpoint, the gift was too large for her to fully take advantage of the tax opportunity.

On the other hand, many people are giving solely from the heart, and if the money is available and not needed by them, then gifts of this size and much greater are still being made, because of need.

Another alternative to an outright gift is a gift that would go toward the establishment of her own Donor Advised Foundation. This foundation would be set up in her family name, but with the expressed instructions that monies are to go to First Congregational Church. These donor-advised accounts are becoming more and more popular. That is why Charitable Alliance Group has chosen this format over the standard, more restrictive, private family foundation.

Fidelity Charitable Gift Fund, out of Boston, Massachusetts, estimates they will raise $5 billion this year in these accounts.

Conclusion

It is our opinion that either an outright gift or a Donor Advised Foundation would best suit Mrs. Smith's needs.

CASE STUDY #2
MRS. JONES

Mrs. Jones has attended a workshop at First Congregational Church. The title of the workshop was Advanced Stewardship. The following was discussed at the workshop:

1. Overview of charitable gifting.
2. What can you give?
3. Restrictions & limitations on giving.
4. Charitable Gifting Strategies.
5. Case Studies.
6. What's next? How you can get involved with First Congregational and Charitable Alliance.

Specifically, Mrs. Jones decides she would like to give stock certificates as a charitable gift. Her concerns are: If she holds onto the stock, what would happen at death? Could her heirs be forced to sell the stock to pay estate taxes? What are the capital gains tax liabilities? Could the stock certificates be tied up in probate?

Case Solution

When gifted to a charitable organization, all gifts of stock, real estate, businesses, collectibles, and so on, will:

- Avoid probate;
- Avoid capital gains tax liability;
- Avoid income tax liability;
- Avoid federal estate tax.

Mrs. Jones may be confused by the many elements involved in setting up a Trust, such as Trustors, Trustees, Legal Purpose, Capacity, Asset Calculation, Heirs, and all the rest.

A simple way to avoid all of these questions and steps in creating a Trust is to *not* create a Trust. Mrs. Jones does not need to create a Trust. She just needs to transfer the assets to the church name and thus she eliminates all of these concerns. Once she has transferred the assets into the name of the church, she has two choices:

1. She can name this gift as an outright gift of stock. The stock must be placed into the name of the church account *first*, and then it can be sold. If the stock is sold first, then she may be subject to capital gains and ordinary income taxes. Once that stock is gifted to the church, the current trading value or market value of the stock will be the amount she can use as a tax deduction. For example: 100,000 shares of ABC Stock, trading at $10 per share, equal a $1million gift . . . and a $1million tax deduction.

2. The same gift can be given to the church, but Mrs. Jones wishes to receive income for life. Charitable Alliance Group will set up a Charitable Gift Annuity. The trustee of the annuity will be First Congregational Church. First Congregational Church will deposit the $1million worth of stock and invest the money in an appropriate investment strategy, which will produce annuity income to Mrs. Jones for the rest of her life. If Mrs. Jones is 65 years old, she can receive approximately 7% for her life remainder, which may go for 20 or 25 years, and she can still deduct a substantial portion of the gift.

What does the church get out of this? The church holds the money in its own foundation account. Charitable Alliance Group as the Administrator constructs a gift annuity. Charitable Alliance Group will make sure that the client receives regular income payments for life. A reserve must be set aside in the amount of 76% of the donated funds. (This is California State law.) There now becomes available $240,000, or 24% of the $1million. A portion of the 24% goes to the church and to the administrator for performing the following services:

- Gift annuity calculations;
- Monthly or quarterly checks;
- Quarterly statements for the clients;
- Securing an institutional co-trustee;
- Performance of all administrative functions along with a possibility of providing a re-insurance that these annuity payments will not be a burden upon the church.

Conclusion

The Charitable Gift Annuity is a good alternative for also naming stocks and bonds held in IRAs and Pension accounts that can also be gifted to the church. The offsetting tax deductions and estate tax savings may solve huge tax obligations that can be incurred when someone dies with an IRA or a pension profit-sharing plan.

CASE STUDY #3

Wealthy Donor looking to give money to the church, receive substantial tax benefits, and pass wealth to heirs.

WIN—WIN—WIN

The biggest problem that all hard-working Americans face is a tax system that is unrelenting and will not stop unless you as an individual can apply the brakes. Unfortunately, the IRS taxes us when we make money, when we save money, and when we die.

The most dramatic example of this is someone who has saved all his or her life to build up a retirement plan, and that retirement plan is a terrible thing to die with! Based on today's current tax laws, heirs who would receive the proceeds from that retirement plan could be taxed higher than 79 cents on the dollar at death. Why is this so high? Estate taxes can reach 55% of the accumulated wealth and ordinary income tax at 39% federal and also applicable state income taxes.

Remember, it's not what you make . . . it's what you keep. There is one thing we all know for sure. If you do no planning at all, Uncle Sam will take what you can't take with you.

Charitable Alliance Group and its staff have over forty years' experience in the areas of advanced charitable gifting, wealth accumulation strategies and wealth transfer strategies. Charitable Alliance Group has designed a ninety-minute workshop titled *Advanced Stewardship*. The concept of "giving with warm hands" or "give while you live" will benefit the charity, the donor and the heirs.

The basic strategies typically take over ninety minutes to fully understand, yet the process can evolve with action being taken by a potential donor within a matter of weeks, and donations can be flowing to the church within the first thirty days or less.

These strategies are time-tested (some have been around for over 130 years), yet they are still somewhat "stealthy" to most people. It is our job to take the stealth and turn it into wealth. Wealth means giving more to the charity, getting more back to the donor, and leaving more to the beneficiaries. (Foundation accounts, The Charitable Gift Annuity, The Wealth Replacement Life Trust, The Win-Win-Win Strategy.)

The Win-Win Goal

The process must specialize in helping highly affluent individuals to achieve maximum financial planning. It will save a large amount on taxes. It will produce a retirement program that will supplement their standard of living. It will preserve wealth for loved ones. Best of all, it will produce the highest maximum results to the charity, so the charity can fulfill its highest growth and outreach aspirations.

CASE STUDY #4
MRS. DOE WITH A STOCK WORTH $425,000

Option: Donate Assets to a Charitable Remainder Trust and Establish a Wealth Replacement Trust

- Avoid Capital Gains Tax upon transfer—the entire $425,000 goes to work.
- Elect a 7% Retirement Account.
- Receive an immediate tax deduction of approximately $133,000 (the present value of the remainder interest), for an actual tax savings of $41,000.
- Over Mrs. Doe's 24-year life expectancy, she will receive more than $774,000 in income.
- At death, approximately $506,000 will go to the Charity of choice (instead of Uncle Sam), while bypassing Mrs. Doe's estate tax.
- Added Strategy: Purchase a Life Insurance Policy using the Income Tax Savings and Increased Income.
- Gift $15,000 per year into a Trust.
- Trust purchase a variable life policy (with $1,000,000 face) for the benefit of her grandchildren.
- Upon Mrs. Doe's death the grandchildren will receive $1,000,000 free from estate, and income taxation.

ASSET REPLACEMENT

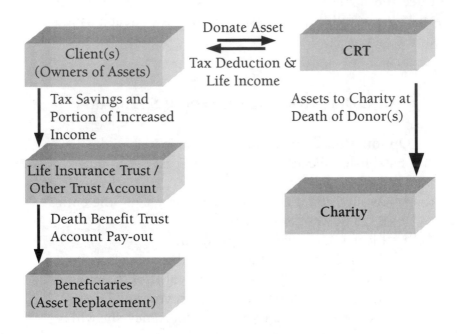

CASE STUDY #5
MR. JAMES

Mr. James is a highly compensated executive who has just been given stock options as an incentive for excellent performance. With these options some problems may arise if the options are:

1. Non-transferable;
2. Lack of diversification;
3. Non-income producing (frequently).

In addition, other problems include:

4. When exercised, the difference between the current market price of the stock and the option's exercise price is taxable at ordinary income tax rates—up to 39.6% federal, plus applicable state taxes—regardless if you sell or hold.
5. Since many individuals are in the top tax bracket already (or the exercise pushes them into the top tax bracket), exercising a large number of options can be very painful from a tax perspective. . . . **so what can Mr. James do?**

The Stock Option / Grantor Charitable Lead Trust Strategy

Step #1
- Mr. James simultaneously exercises the non-qualified stock options and sells the underlying stock.
- Taxable income = the number of options exercised, multiplied by the market price of the stock on the date of exercise, minus the option price.

Step #2
- Mr. James irrevocably transfers the cash profit from the stock sale to a Charitable Lead Trust (the transfer can also be stock/bonds) and sets the distribution percentage and term of the trust.
- The trust reinvests the cash into securities that may be either taxable or tax-free.
- Mr. James receives an up-front tax deduction for the present value of the income stream gifted to charity. (Must be Grantor Lead Trust)

- $ Amount x # of years x Present Value Factor.

Step #3
- Mr. James uses the up-front tax deduction generated by the Charitable Lead Trust to offset the taxable income associated with the exercise of the non-qualified stock options. (Must be Grantor Lead Trust)
- Up to 30% ceiling of AGI in tax year.

Step #4
- The CLT distributes monies to the charity for a designated term. The income distributed each year is generally taxable to Mr. James.
- One exception is when the CLT invests in tax-exempt municipal bonds.

Step #5
- At the end of the trust term, the trust corpus and undistributed income revert back to Mr. James or pass to other designated non-charitable beneficiaries such as the client's children or grandchildren— avoids probate and passes estate-tax free. (There might be gift taxes on the monies passed to heirs at the time the trust is established.)

CALCULATE POTENTIAL CHARITABLE DEDUCTION FROM THE CLT

Fair Market Value of assets placed into CLT:	$1,000,000
Income Distribution:	x 8%
Annual Distribution to Charity	$80,000
Trust Term in Years:	x 10
Total Distributions to Charity:	$800,000
PV of Total Distributions to Charity:	$595,000*

(*Approximate, assuming an IRS section 7520 rate of 5.8%)

CALCULATE OFFSET

Taxable Income Generated by Option Exercise: $1,000,000
Up-front Charitable Deduction from CLT*   -595,000
Net Taxable Income   **$405,000**
(*In general, the charitable deduction is limited to 30% of AGI. Any unused portion subjects to five-year carry forward rule).

Stock Option / CLT Strategy

- Five-year carry forward of remaining tax deduction (also subject to 30% AGI limitation in following tax years).
- Size of CLT charitable deduction depends on several factors which include:
  - Fair Market Value of assets transferred to the trust
  - Term of the trust
  - Charity's income distribution percentage
  - Applicable IRS federal interest rate

With the CLT the taxable income is $405,000
Without the CLT the taxable income is $1,000,000

Stock's Fair Market Value/share	$40
Exercise Price	-20
Taxable Element	$20
Number of Options Exercised	x 50,000
Taxable Income	$1,000,000
Federal Tax Rate	x 39.6%
Tax Liability of Option Exercise	$396,000*

(* Does not include state income tax, if any)

SUMMARY OF BENEFITS

- Client gets tax deduction to offset option exercise.
- Trust corpus returns to client or passes to heirs avoiding estate and probate taxes, at stepped up cost basis. (May be subject to gift taxes)
- Client enjoys the benefit of seeing the results of a charitable gift during his or her lifetime.
- Client avoids the capital gain on the stock option exercise.

CONCLUSION

The client is able to keep more of his Financial Capital and his Social Capital due to the above strategy. Without this technique the U.S. government would have been "the charity but not of choice."

❧ *Chapter Nine* ☙

NOTABLE QUOTES

These are some of my favorite quotations, which are not so much politically correct as they are charitably correct:

"Science and technology are climbing the mountain of mystery, and they will find when they reach the top that faith was waiting the whole time.."

—Peter O'Toole

"The greatest good you can do for another is not just share your riches, but to reveal to him his own."

—Benjamin Disraeli

"Goodness is easier to recognize than it is to define."

—W.H. Auden

"Without Humility there can be no humanity."

—Don Buchan

"Throw your heart over the fence and the rest will follow."

—Norman Vincent Peale

"Friendship is a single soul dwelling in two bodies."
—Aristotle

"Friendship is your option, Stewardship is not."
—Mitch Morrison

"Let us not look back in anger or forward in fear, but around in awareness."
—James Thurber

"My definition of gratitude is: if I had to do it all over again, I would do it all over again."
—Mitch Morrison

"When you drink the water remember the stream."
—Chinese proverb

"A life is not important except for the impact it has on other lives."
—Jackie Robinson

"You can preach a better sermon with your life than with your lips."
—Oliver Goldsmith

"A Father is much more than a Human Being to his son."
—Thomas William Simpson

"If there is no wind, row!"
—Latin Proverb

"If you don't know where you're going, you will wind up somewhere else."
—Yogi Berra

"Charity is a contact sport; you have to make contact."
—Mitch Morrison

"Don't just learn the tricks of the trade, learn the trade."
—James Bennis

"It's what you learn after you know it all that counts."
—John Wooden

"Things turn out best for those who make the best of the way things turn out."
—Daniel Considine

"Planned Giving? What I need is Planned Getting!"
—Pastor Bill Wilson

"What is a charitable gift? If you lose your luggage at the airport that was probably a charitable gift! Somebody else probably benefits and you can take a tax deduction."
—Mitch Morrison

THIS LAST QUOTE IS MY PERSONAL FAVORITE:

"The Ark was built by amateurs;
The Titanic was built by professionals."

THE CHECK

In my hand I hold this check
It's not that much but what the heck
I prayed this passion would appear
I'll give more, maybe next year

I've slipped under compassion's spell
Not sure it keeps me from fires of Hell
My life has not been quite the same
Since I began this giving game

Feeling renewed as I pledge this gift
I beg it gives all hope a lift
Some can judge if I've made a dent
It's God's eyes my message was sent

I know this quest is not just a whim
It's time for all to come join in
Who gave the most when all was done
The answer must be—there's more than one

—Mitch Morrison

OUR PRAYER

Lord we follow your Word as the absolute truth. Give us
the courage to keep faith to Your will, knowing the forces
of evil attempt to prevent this. The road You direct us to
travel will lead us from the great darkness and into the great
light. We know you will never leave us or forsake us and
when we have finally reached our journey's end our lives
were fulfilled because we worked and lived to fulfill the
lives of others.

—Mitch Morrison

❧ Chapter Ten ❧

ALLIANCE CHARITIES

Foundations working with other Foundations
to maximize the end result:
People Helping People

The Charitable Alliance concept creates a simple formula. In the perfect world, all things would not only be possible but actually would be obtainable on a regular basis. In the perfect world, a natural alliance would exist with everyone lacking nothing. This would mean decisions would not have to be made and no worthy cause would lack for resources. Perhaps the word "capital" has more meaning than we realize. Capitalism is really the only true source of resources.

The Alliance brings out the notion that capitalism in its purest form will not work in charity. Capitalism always entails competition and the strong ruling over the weak. Instead, we must prepare to take on the challenge of serving and not competing. Arguably, funds may not be better spent with collaboration of multiple charities; however, it may create more resources if charities *would* collaborate their resources. For example, instead of a large donor doling out small contributions to an assortment of various causes, it would be wiser for charities to combine their resources toward a single shared project that would have a greater impact on a specific need. In the business world this is known as taking advantage of economies of scale.

So what is the bottom line? Could it be possible that charities could actually help each other out through a barter system? Could they combine their resources and accomplish more, help more people with greater impact? My company, Charitable Alliance Group, believes this is the case. This is why the new philanthropy will be the driving force behind strategies fulfilling community and goodwill.

Specifically, a charity such as NFL Legends was created to help ex-NFL players who are in dire need. Dire need means: ill health, poor financial condition, or debilitating handicaps such as crippling arthritis, senile dementia, and Alzheimer's. NFL Legends has been able to raise significant funds through an alliance group, yet was still looking for a site to purchase. Another Charitable Alliance client (The Joshua Tree Center of Spiritual Healing) was looking for money to refurbish and enhance their 62-year-old facility. The end result was simple. We put the money with the land and buildings, and are in the process of consummating the first-ever NFL Legends Village. This is a non-profit village, which will derive continuing support from National Football League owners, players and sponsors.

The term "new philanthropy" does not describe *how* people are donating money; it describes how *charities* can best combine new ideas and resources, resulting in how this money is utilized. If a charitable organization has a resource and a different charity has a resource, even though their directions of service are varied it may work out that by combining resources both charities can be served.

Strategic alliances are common in business and seem to be a foregone conclusion when it comes to the Internet. Part of the lifeblood of the Internet seems to be the "Links" pages. Relationships are the key to success and the key to momentum. Some charities have a fear of sharing their power or domain with other causes. That's one of the mistakes charities are making today. Things do move fast in the business world, and if you're not cutting edge most of the time, you're going to be left behind. Remember, every volunteer you sign-up, every donation you receive, every resource your foundation or charity has is valuable. This means that at one point in time, one man's trash is another man's treasure. Look at what is available to offer. Research what might be valuable. In our multicultural age it makes sense to look at the advantages and opportunities of forming partnerships. There is a lot happening out there you do not know about. It is impossible to keep abreast if you're not actively seeking new contacts and resources.

The community you live in may embrace the barter system. A lot of ideas come from small business and local people. Your first objective should be to get to know those people and let them get to know you. Financial modernization today may be running at its highest efficiency level ever in the United States. The investors who seek the questions, "Tell me what's going on, how can I become a successful investor in a short period?" did become successful investors. What was the secret? They listened to others and others were willing to share information, ideas and experience. Charitable organizations must do the same thing. The New Charity demands cooperation. As discussed previously, "social Darwinism" has no place in charity. The strong must not rule the weak. The strong must share with the weak. This is the basis of charitable modernization.

Creating more assets for our charitable community is not only a concern but also a necessary goal if we are to keep our society healthy. The ability to create economic strength in our communities, within our churches and our neighborhood centers, is vital. It revolves around trusting each other more and capitalizing on our own intellectual commodity.

Politics may drive our nation, but it will be the people who drive our community. The people we choose to empower, the people who chose to refrain from involvement, these will make all the difference. The one who is walking around asking, "What's going on?" is not going to be much help in today's world. Forward thinking and envisioning, which will improve for the coming generations, will be the most important contributions. These contributions require leaders and volunteers that place issues at the forefront of their own personal agenda. It is a free country and everyone is free to exercise his or her passion; however, the personal agenda wears thin. The strength in the organization will come from new alliances and relationships that produce results. Charities must have a plan, revisit that plan from time-to-time, and share the plan with others. Diversity is the best defense against adversity.

ALLIANCE CHARITIES
Finding Ways That Improve the World

In life many things change and many things remain. Opportunities will change and also remain the same. The principals remain constant: Buying, selling, trading. These are the true things that bring in resources. They are also the same principals that create the "haves" and "have-nots." The big picture is often overlooked, or at least partially lost when commerce is ignored. Buying, selling and trading are what will create opportunity in charity, as it does in business. Having a strong passion or resolve will also create opportunity, yet the ability to let business roll on will make all the difference.

The biggest mistake most charities continue to make is that they sit and wait for something to happen. They may rely on false promises and not focus on consistent daily activity that will bring in dollars and resources.

The process that must take place should have momentum and focus. Focus is the ability to see a need and the passion for the need, put together at the same time. It is great to expose the need yourself, yet people must follow this passion in an equal effort. Passion is based on the decision to see the need clearly and criteria for the process of fulfilling the need. Focus is the same disciplined process that affects business, or more specifically, investments. If a charity and its focus can be identified with opportunity that makes sense, then successful results will occur. Everyone will be required to move beyond inspiration to perspiration.

Remember, when people invest, they look for opportunity and the end result is a reward system that is time-tested. Money is the result of a successful investment. Or, to be exact, having more money than someone started with makes for a successful investment. The degree of success in a charity is the most difficult to quantify. The charity should be mission-driven and values-based on a greater good that can and will take place. Goals should be measured by the creation of a meaningful impact: Performance is related to both perspiration and the ability to gain advantages. In charity, we must look at performance in a different light. This light is not based on beating the competition; it's based on cooperation and the combining of resources.

The Infrastructure for the "New Charity" for the 21st Century

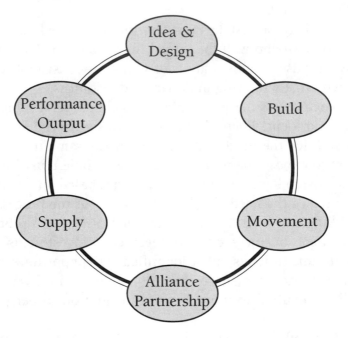

The ability for charities to create and maintain alliance partnerships will definitely affect their ability to succeed in the near future. The old adage "Two heads are better than one" can work quite well in charity. Today, charities are seeking out business partners to help with their causes, and businesses are looking for charities that they can work with to show the public what they stand for.

What Process Makes for a Successful Charity?

Idea generation tends to lead the way. The key is momentum. The momentum can come from either a positive or a negative event. However, the momentum will only be sustained if the need is being met with results. The reason why a charity can only sustain the negative momentum for so long is that if the charity was founded due to a tragic event (example: Mothers Against Drunk Driving), then the momentum must move toward solving the problem. If MADD only continues to expose individual drunk driving cases, then the negative consumes the positive, and the momentum shifts. In this case I am only using MADD as an example. MADD has developed many pro-active focus programs to deter drunk drivers. The progression of a group like MADD is really the way a charity should evolve. If the public sees the positive results dominating the negative, then support grows. The negative event will get everyone's attention, but real dollars will be raised because the charity is making a difference.

Look for charities that can identify opportunities or ideas before they become commonplace or mundane. At Charitable Alliance, we focus to develop four characteristics for our alliance charities. They are:

1. CHANGE. Any charity that can bring about some true change is really going to get strong momentum in its favor. When the issues or problems are in flux, then the change can take place in a more rapid manner. Anyone can make a gripe; not everyone has the talent and commitment to make a difference which will result in changes taking place.
2. THEMES. Charities that will gain momentum are the ones that are moving with a theme. These themes must

move with and not against the major social, economic and cultural shifts taking place in the world.

3. **FRANCHISE**. I know this sounds like a stretch, but look at what people are buying today. People look for brand names and availability. It's not so much that bigger is better, but "everywhere is better." The brand name is leveraged through franchises. Growth with a charitable cause can come through carefully managed franchise extensions in new areas of the country. Remember, the goal is also to build momentum. By franchising, momentum can build.

4. **NATIONAL OR GLOBAL REACH**. Leverage and national attention go hand-in-hand. There are many ways to increase reach: media attention, publicity, endorsement from famous people, planning an event (which is also covered by the media), and just getting the word out on what you are doing. In many cases, luck can have its way. It could be something that is planned or something that just happens to draw attention and reach. It is very important not to let positive events falter. Charities must learn to capitalize.

How can a charity utilize principals in business to create opportunities for itself? As previously stated, charity is not a business, and there are many things about charitable fundamentals that make them different from fundamentals in business. However, the criteria for judging a charity's effectiveness and potential is very similar to the principles applied in analysis of companies and their stock price or their growth potential.

If you are familiar with the concepts of top-down analysis and bottom-up analysis, you will understand the logic that can be used in assessing a charity. The company may become a buy or sell based on a rigorous and highly disciplined analytic process involving macro- and micro-economic factors. This analysis forms the basis of the decision by an investment professional or securities analyst who makes his living buying and selling stocks.

Top-Down Analysis. The macro analytic process creates a social, economic and political climate against which companies are viewed. The same can be applied toward individual charities. Macro analysis includes consideration of global trends affecting interest rates, inflation, regulations, and the competition. Top-down analysis also means the overall economy, industry analysis, operating trends, shift in attitudes and sustainability of trends.

Bottom-Up Analysis. Bottom-up analysis means modeling all aspects of a company and can be applied toward individual charities to see how they size up. This approach will target the company, the individuals, and so forth. The whole company is under the microscope, not just the company's stock. The goal in the bottom-up process is an in-depth knowledge of all internal aspects of the company or charity, particularly management. This analysis specifically considers management commitment to enhancing value to the company. In our charitable example, one looks for management's commitment to building momentum and efficient operations that produce measurable results.

What do top-down and bottom-up mean to someone who is looking for a good charity to support? It could mean everything and nothing at the same time. If that person who wishes to do his homework on a charity bases his decision on the efficiency and management of the charity, then bottom-up is very important. If another person views the overall visions and cause of the charity to be most important, then the top-down approach is best. Either way, both could be the right answer. The perfect scenario is having both strong administration/management and a strong cause that is supported by a trend in society. The cause may even be in fashion, so to speak.

A successful campaign in regards to a charity will have a need, show a movement, provide solutions and be able to utilize the resources in an efficient manner. Because charity is about giving, then giving can be a two-way street. The charities themselves must give or share impact with groups that support it. It would be foolish to ignore image and initiatives that may be desired by a corporation when it supports a charity of choice. Causes, it has been argued, are as good for a company's bottom line as they are for society at large. In a study produced by Roper-Starch, a New York City research firm, and Core, Inc., of Boston, it was revealed that nearly two-thirds (61%) of retail consumers said that when price and quality are equal, they would be likely to switch to retailers or brands that are associated with a good cause. And even better news . . . a whopping 68% said they would pay more for a product from a company linked to a good cause.

"The bottom line impact can be very real, and it can also be very significant for a company's marketing success," says Carol Core, CEO, Core, Inc. The 1999 Core/Roper Cause-Related Trends Report, a five-year analysis of cause marketing trends said, "Two-thirds of the people surveyed (66%) had greater trust in those companies aligned with a social cause."

Who Are the Charitable Companies?

STARBUCKS

This Seattle-based coffee retailer is definitely making a difference. Starbucks actually employs a full-time Senior

Vice President of Corporate Social Responsibility. Dave Olson is in charge of community efforts and charitable giving. The Starbucks Foundation was formed in 1997 with an initial $500,000 from the company founder, Howard Schultz. This company has been the largest annual North American corporate contributor to the international relief organizations since 1991. Starbucks has rolled out a new employee initiative: Make Your Mark. The program is designed to honor employee volunteerism. The company will match an associate's volunteer hours with dollars to the same organization.

WAL-MART

Wal-Mart will donate $160 million this year at the community level through "Good Works," a mix of corporate contributions, gifts, donations from employees and consumers. The company encourages employee volunteerism and public awareness, and provides grants. The program is grassroots and community-based. The great thing about Wal-Mart is the get-it-done attitude that is prevalent at both management and worker levels. In this case it was charity that brought management and store employees together. This could start a trend in labor relations for all companies.

BEN & JERRY'S

Ben & Jerry's gives back 7.5% of its pre-tax earnings to the community. Yes . . . you heard it right: *pre-tax* earnings! This amount has earned Ben & Jerry's a very distinctive place in American business. The company placed first in social responsibility in a 1999 public opinion survey of corporate image, conducted by Harris Inter-Active and the Reputation Institute, a New York City research group. Ben & Jerry's enjoys one of the highest profiles around when it comes to combining a social mission with company success.

The focus is directed toward grassroots community organizations. The program is called *Partner Shop* and establishes local stores in a partnership with non-profit organizations that offer job training to underprivileged youth and adults. The company will waive the standard franchise fees in order for a non-profit group to become an owner-operator of a Ben & Jerry's store. The business profits of these stores are utilized to help support the charitable program. In New York City, Ben & Jerry's partnered with Common Ground Community, a group dedicated to ending homelessness. Currently they have two stores operating as Partner Shops with that group. This looks like a program that really works!

TARGET CORPORATION

Target Corporation, formerly the Dayton Hudson Corporation, has a long track record when it comes to philanthropy. Since 1946 it has given .5% of its annual federally taxable income to charities. In 1997 Target took on a local challenge of helping education. This program is called "Take Charge of Education." The initiative is a school-funding program in which the Target charge-card holders can designate 1% of their in-store or on-line card purchases to a school of their choice. This rebate program and the generous giving at the corporate level have really made a difference in many lives. Target says they will give back more than $1 million a week to local communities with the "Take Charge of Education" program.

Above is not a complete list. These companies are prime examples of what can be and is being done, however. The best businesses and their charitable programs keep repeating themselves. It is good for business to show its customers and partners its commitment to something other than the almighty buck. The customer will be impressed with a business that can show it stands for something! In the years to come, consumers, customers, employees and investors are not only going to ask what the company makes that earns profits. They will also ask, "What are you contributing to make a difference?"

The charitable responsibility that has been dominant at Ben & Jerry's, Starbucks, Home Depot, Wal-Mart, Target Corporation and many other organizations is giving people a reason to do business with them. Charities can learn a lesson and get involved in this trend of "cause marketing" that is taking the place of regular marketing. These programs help a business take steps to receive a higher profile. The result is a differentiation to their brand and image enhancement that goes far beyond simply writing a charitable check.

A charity can actually give back in this regard. It can provide a supporting business partner with employee pride, loyalty, and increased commitment to the company from its consumers or customers. The charity can bring in favorable publicity, which allows both the company and the charity to stand out. Charity must encourage the traditional corporate giving to move to a broader concept of corporate activism. "The New Charity" will see more and more companies walking the walk before they talk the talk. This means they must go out and actually *do* something before they *promise* to do something.

(Source: B.S.R.—Business of Social Responsibility, San Francisco, CA)

ALLIANCE CHARITIES

Arena Group Foundation
Ernie Hahn, Director
3500 Sports Arena Blvd.
San Diego, CA 92130

Athletes for Education Foundation
Carolyn Kelderman, Stephen Haynes
P.O. Box 900517
San Diego, CA 92190

Bill Walton's South Mission Beach Sports Park
Bruk Vandeweghe, Director
1010 University Ave. #1010
San Diego, CA 92103

C.A.U.S.E.
Christian Athletes United for Spiritual Empowerment
Karen Baynard, Admin. Coordinator
3400 Park Avenue
Minneapolis, MN 55407
www.christianathletes.com

Children's Miracle Network
Kendra Howell, Director, Children's Miracle Network
Salinas Valley Memorial Hospital
450 E. Ronnie Lane
Salinas, CA 93901

Claude Crabb Foundation
Claude Crabb, President
755 San Simeon Dr.
Salinas, CA 93901

C.U.G.M.
Churches Uniting in Global Mission
Chet Tolson, Executive Director
P.O. Box 1665
Apple Valley, CA 92307
Website: www.cugm.com

Cypress Community Church
Wayne Adams, Pastor
P.O. Box 3170
Monterey, CA 93942
Website: www.cypresschurch.org

Feed God's Children
Dr. F. Kenton Beshore, Director
P.O. Box 5000
Costa Mesa, CA 92628

Foundation Trilogy
Thomas Winn, Director
3040 Post Oak Blvd., Ste. 675
Houston, TX 77056

Foundation for Wisdom on Wealth
David Roth, Director
1811 E. Garry Ave.
Santa Ana, CA 92705

Garden Grove National Junior Basketball
P.O. Box 754
Garden Grove, CA 92842

Healing Souls for Christ Foundation
Barry Brown, Director
22612 Revere Rd.
Lake Forest, CA 92630

The HILL Foundation
Scott Faber, Asst. Director
PMB 224, 2705 61st Street, Suite B
Galveston, TX 77551-1866

Hog Heaven Foundation
Kris Friedrich, Director
10 Charlotte
Irvine, CA 92612

Homeless Ventures
Marty Jensen, Director
919 Manhattan, Suite F-103
Manhattan Beach, CA 90266

First Congregational Church of Los Angeles
Dr. Steven Berry, Sr. Minister
540 S. Commonwealth Ave.
Los Angeles, CA 90020
Website: www.FCCLA.org

International Bible College
Dennis Jones, President
P.O. Box IBC
3625 Helton Dr.
Florence, AL 35630
Website: www.i-b-c.edu

John Brown University
James L. Krall, Ed.D.
2000 Western University Street
Siloam Springs, AR 72761
Website: www.jbu.edu

Joshua Tree Center
Paul Burkett, Director
P.O. Box 1000
Joshua Tree, CA 92252-0887

Gale Lawrence Foundation
Dr. Gale Lawrence, Director
1600 Pacific Coast Hwy.
Seal Beach, CA 90740

Mariners Church—High School Ministries
5001 Newport Coast Drive
Irvine, CA 92612
Website: www.marinerschurch.org

Missing & Exploited Children (National Center for)
California Branch
18111 Irvine Blvd.
Tustin, CA 92780
Website: www.onederlandpress.com

Minnie Street Learning Center
A community outreach of Lighthouse Ministries—Mariners Church
Rebecca Bramlett, Laurie Beshore, Directors
1010 S. Minnie Street #3
Santa Ana, CA 92701
Website: www.marinerschurch.org
(See: Lighthouse Local Outreach)

Miracles-In-Motion
A community outreach of Lighthouse Ministries—
Mariners Church
Holiday Zimmerman, Director
5001 Newport Coast Dr.
Irvine, CA 92612

New Life Ministry, Ukraine
Anatoly I. Kaluzhni, Chairman
5a, Miltchakova str.
253002 Kiev, Ukraine
Contact: gmolway@marinerschurch.org

NFL Legends (Dire Needs Fund)
Sophie Morrison, Director
1335 Aveneda Sereno
Encinitas, CA 92024Website:
www.nfl.com

O'Shea Foundation
Michael O'Shea, Founder
858 Ocean Ave.
Sea Bright, NJ 07760

Project Love
Reggie Bibbes, Director
4th Ave. #514
San Diego, CA 92101

Robert Griffith Foundation
Katrina Leonce, Executive Director
3999 Austell Rd., Sute 303
Austell, GA 30001
Email: GriffsGoal@aol.com

S.A.V.E.
Students Against Violence in Education
Bill Calder, Director
273 Marchmont Dr.
Los Gatos, CA 95032

Tabernacle of Praise
John Wynn, Pastor
Sacramento, CA

The Sports Coach Charitable Alliance Foundation
Gordon Brown & Eric Galtress, Directors
5325 N. Commerce Ave. #2
Moorpark, CA 93021

Tiger Creek Foundation
Abby & Emma Hedengran, Directors
45305 Calle Cuero
Temecula, CA 92590
Email: tigercreek@direcpc.com

USA Youth Golf Foundation
Damon DeVito, Director
355 Peter Jefferson Place, Ste. 100
Charlottesville, VA 22911

United States Golf Fitness Association
Larry Castro, Director
2246 Orange Grove Place
Escondido, CA 92027
Website: www.usgfa.com

World Bible Society
Dr. F. Kenton Beshore, Director
P.O. Box 5000
Costa Mesa, CA 92628

Chapter Eleven

WHO ARE THE
IMPOSTERS OF CHARITY?

How can you know if you, personally, are an imposter of charity? If you are really willing to look at your own degree of passion: give yourself a simple test.

First, get out your checkbook ledger and go through the last six months of checks written. Count the number of checks that went to social causes or any charitable functions you attended. If nothing shows up, then you may not be practicing what you preach.

Second, take out your daily or weekly planner and look where you have or haven't been. Does that check reveal anything other than shopping, personal trainer, spa, Harley Davidson repairs and service, boat payments, or other spending for yourself? The checkbook and the schedule planner may painfully reveal that you take on very few charitable responsibilities, nor do you regularly give to charities.

For those of you who wish to put more thought into a self-evaluation on philanthropy, The New Charity has prepared a "charity test" which you may take and grade yourself. Keep in mind, take this test honestly and remember: bats aren't actually blind; wolves don't howl at the moon; owls aren't wise; and denial ain't just a river in Egypt. (Get it? "De Nile")

Take the Imposters of Charity Test:

1. When it comes to charity, would you prefer to:
   A. Let the government take care of all needs.
   B. Get involved in my later years.
   C. Give only to the largest national charities.
   D. Do research and find out which causes are making a difference.
2. I have volunteered or worked for a charity:
   A. Never
   B. Once or Twice
   C. I belong to a group, which is a charity or supports charity.
   D. I am a volunteer or a regular giver.
3. When it comes to my tax dollars, I believe the following:
   A. The government has done an excellent job meeting all human needs.
   B. The local city or town can and will provide for all its people with social services.
   C. Social services should be earned, not based on need.
   D. Charitable contributions must continue to rise in order to fill in the gaps not provided by state or federal government.
4. When it comes to our kids:

A. Our children go to church or temple on a regular basis, and have been involved in outreach programs; or, we don't worship, but we encourage our children to volunteer.

B. We have our own charities we support, but our kids aren't involved.

C. We have not encouraged our children to learn about philanthropy or volunteer work.

D. We would prefer to let them decide later, when they are adults.

5. This is my opinion regarding a Family Foundation:

A. This is a tax haven for only the very wealthy.

B. I can't do as much in strategic giving or the timing of my gifts without my own foundation or donor advised account.

C. Lawyers, accountants and advisors will be necessary and very expensive if I start a Family Foundation.

D. It is better to wait until later in life to start a Family Foundation or donor-directed account.

6. Which of the following statements is not a TRUE statement:

A. Every 56 seconds, a baby is born in the United States without health insurance.

B. One in three children in the U.S. will be poor at some point in their childhood.

C. Tennessee and Texas rank highest in children's social services and rights.

D. Every 40 seconds a baby is born into poverty in the U.S.

7. Three people are wandering in a New York City subway station, panhandling. Who do you think deserves the money?

A. The homeless woman with the sign, "Help me hire a hit man to kill my husband."

B. The homeless man carrying a sign that reads: "Why lie? I need a beer!"

C. The homeless man, whose sign says, "Tell me off! One dollar!"

D. All of them deserve the money. There is no bad giving.

(Answers on page 192)

THE IMPOSTERS OF CHARITY

Only three things count in the true assessment of charity and giving. *How much* was actually given in money, food, supplies or support? *Who received it?* Did all of it go to the needy? *How fast* did the money or goods fulfill the needs?

• How much?
• Who got it?
• How long did it take?

The message I give to the Venture Philanthropist is: "Stop wasting your time." There is no bad giving. What is it about that statement you don't understand? It doesn't count if you don't give it out. I don't care how much you currently have in your Foundation. I don't care how your research has developed a filter system to deny charities that aren't worthy. When you are asked how much is in your Foundation, you should say, "I hope nothing. I hope we've given it all out!"

A recent story in *Time* magazine featured the "New Philanthropists." The article states, "They're hands-on, they want results, and they're doing their homework!"

The hidden story was not actually revealed in the *Time* magazine article, March 24, 2000, however. The article listed the top twelve philanthropists living in the United States:

1. BILL & MELINDA GATES, Redmond, Washington
    $22 Billion given or pledged
    Time cover story: Source of wealth: Microsoft Co-Founder
    Beneficiaries include: Bill & Melinda Gates Foundation, which finances international vaccinations and children's health programs.

    Undercover Story: Given or pledged $22 billion. The question here is not the pledge part, but the given part. This foundation became very rich quickly, but is giving its money away slowly. For example, slightly less than $400 million a year goes for global health causes and the other given part has been donations relating to computers and software to upgrade libraries and public facilities. Thanks to the foundation, 22,530 computers have been wired in the U.S. and 4,024 have been wired in Canada. Interesting that MicroSoft also sells to computer owners. The foundation director states that their actual goal is to give out $1 billion per year. That's 4.5% of the corpus per year.

    In Bill's defense, he has still given away money faster than anyone before his time, but on a relative scale, this foundation could give much more and faster.
2. GEORGE SOROS, New York City
    $2 billion given or pledged.
    Time cover story: Source of wealth—Hedge Fund manager. Beneficiaries include: Soros Foundation Network, Children's programs, public health programs, contem-

porary artistic and cultural programs, small enterprise development.

Undercover story: Actual dollars given to charitable programs were not available through the source of this article.

3. TED TURNER, Atlanta, Georgia
    $1.385 Billion given or pledged
    Time **cover story**: Source of wealth: CNN Founder, Time-Warner Vice Chairman. Beneficiaries include: U.N. Foundation and Turner Foundation. Supports international children's health and environmental programs.

    Undercover story: The pledged part of this equation is very interesting. Ted Turner formed a Charitable Lead Trust, which is discussed in this book. A lead trust should not be confused with an outright gift. The established lead trust of $1 billion by Turner actually gives out only $50 million per year, or 5% of the amount stated in the *Time* article. There are favorable tax advantages to having your own lead trust and a great deal of control by the donor.

4. JAMES E. (Jr.) & VIRGINIA G. STOWERS, Kansas City, Missouri
    $360 million given or pledged.

5. PAUL ALLEN, Mercer Island, Washington
    $355 million given or pledged.

6. JON HURTSMAN, Salt Lake City, Utah
    $350 million given or pledged.

7. PATRICK J. McGOVERN & LORE HARP-McGOVERN, San Francisco, CA
    $350 million given or pledged.

8. MARTHA R. INGRAM, Nashville, Tennessee

$300 million given or pledged.
9. ALFRED MANN, Beverly Hills, California
   $270 million given or pledged.
10. KIRK KERKORIAN, Los Angeles, California
    $250 million given or pledged.
11. DAVE & CHERYL DUFFIELD, Lake Tahoe, Nevada
    $220 million given or pledged.
12. JAMES E. ROGERS, Las Vegas, Nevada
    $208.7 million given or pledged.

Big Players in the dot-com and high-tech field have been stealth givers:

1. LAWRENCE ELLISON, CEO of Oracle
   Estimated to be worth around $50 billion, he claims to give around $100 million per year. That's .05% or 1/2 cent on his dollars per year. His largest single contribution outside his foundation was $5 million to the University of California at Davis. Again, only 1/1000 of a cent on the dollars he is worth.
2. STEVE CASE, Chairman, AOL
   He claims he has given $200 million over the past five years.
3. JEFF BEZOS, Founder, Amazon
   He declines to say how much he gives.
4. JERRY YANG, Co-Founder, Yahoo
   He says he gives actively, but declines to say how much he gives or to whom.
5. MICHAEL DELL, CEO, Dell Computers
   He says he gives actively to children's causes, but declines to say how much he gives, or to whom.
6. MEY WHITMAN, CEO, eBay
   She declines to say how much she gives or to whom.

7. JOHN CHAMBERS, CEO, Cisco Systems
    He says he gives to educational causes, but declines to
    say how much he gives or to whom.
8. DAVID FILO, Co-Founder, Yahoo
    He says he gives actively, but declines to say how much
    he gives or to whom.

THE STORY NEVER TOLD

In Brooklyn, New York, Chush is a school that caters to
learning disabled children. Some children remain in Chush
for their entire school career, while others can be
mainstreamed into conventional schools. At a Chush fundraising dinner, the father of a Chush child delivered a speech
that would never be forgotten by all that attended.

After extolling the school and its dedicated staff, he cried
out, "Where is the perfection in my son, Shaya? Everything
God does is done with perfection. But my child cannot
understand things as other children do. My child cannot
understand facts and figures as other children do. Where is
God's perfection?"

The audience was shocked by the question, pained by
the father's anguish and stilled by the piercing query. "I
believe," the father answered, "that when God brings a child
like this into the world, the perfection that He seeks is in
the way people react to this child." Then he told the following story about his son, Shaya:

One afternoon, Shaya and his father walked past a park
where some boys Shaya knew were playing baseball. Shaya
asked, "Do you think they will let me play?"

Shaya's father knew that his son was not at all athletic
and that most boys would not want him on their team. But
Shaya's father understood that if his son were chosen to

play, it would give him a comfortable sense of belonging. Shaya's father approached one of the boys in the field and asked if Shaya could play.

The boy looked around for guidance from his teammates. Getting none, he took matters into his own hands and said, "We are losing by six runs and the game is in the eighth inning. I guess he can be on our team and we'll try to put him up to bat in the ninth inning."

Shaya's father was ecstatic as Shaya smiled broadly. Shaya was told to put on a glove and go out to play short center field. In the bottom of the eighth inning, Shaya's team scored a few runs but was still behind by three. In the bottom of the ninth inning, Shaya's team scored again and now with two outs and the bases loaded, the potential winning run was on base. Shaya was scheduled to be up. Would the team actually let Shaya bat at this juncture and give away their chance to win the game?

Surprisingly, Shaya was given the bat. Everyone knew that it was all but impossible because Shaya didn't even know how to hold the bat properly, let alone hit with it! However, as Shaya stepped up to the plate, the pitcher moved a few steps to lob the ball in softly so Shaya could at least be able to make contact.

The first pitch came and Shaya swung clumsily and missed. One of Shaya's teammates came up to Shaya and together they held the bat and faced the pitcher waiting for the next pitch. The pitcher again took a few steps forward to toss the ball softly toward Shaya. As the pitch came in, Shaya and his teammate swung at the ball and together they hit a slow ground ball to the pitcher.

The pitcher picked up the soft grounder and could easily have thrown the ball to the first baseman. Shaya would have been out and that would have ended the game.

Instead, the pitcher took the ball and threw it on a high arc to right field, far beyond reach of the first baseman. Everyone started yelling, "Shaya, run to first! Run to first!"

Never in his life had Shaya run to first. He scampered down the baseline, wide-eyed and startled. By the time he reached first base, the right fielder had the ball. He could have thrown the ball to the second baseman, who would tag out Shaya, who was still running. But the right fielder understood what the pitcher's intentions were, so he threw the ball high and far over the third baseman's head. Everyone yelled, "Run to second! Run to second!" Shaya ran toward second base as the runners ahead of him deliriously circled the bases towards home.

As Shaya reached second base, the opposing shortstop ran to him, turned him in the direction of third base and shouted, "Run to third!" As Shaya rounded third the boys from both teams ran behind him screaming, "Shaya, run home!" Shaya ran home, stepped on home plate, and all 18 boys lifted him on their shoulders and made him the hero, as he had just hit a "grand slam" and won the game for his team.

"That day," said the father softly with tears now rolling down his face, "those eighteen boys reached their level of God's perfection."

Funny how stories like this never get published. Funny how our society is not interested in hearing about classmates caring for each other. Funny how this is so true, and shame on us! Funny how simple it is for people to trash different ways of living and believing, and then wonder why the world is going to hell. Funny how morals, beliefs, religion and prayers take a back seat to stories of murder, rape, sex and celebrities.

Funny how you can send a thousand jokes by e-mail and they spread like wildfire, but when you start sending messages regarding life choices, people think twice about sharing. Funny how the lewd, crude, vulgar and obscene pass freely through cyberspace, but the public discussion of morality is suppressed in the school and workplace. Funny, isn't it? Are you laughing?
—Anonymous e-mail

This story has never been shared outside the school. No one published it or wrote about it.

In order to avoid being an imposter of charity, you must not be afraid to share your passion and your spirit. It is not a matter of being pushy but one of resolve. Without resolve, there is no direction. Morals will play a big part, yet "therein is the rub." You may "suffer the slings and arrows." Don't cast judgments, yet stick to your beliefs.

On the other hand, the most devastating imposter is the one in the role of all-powerful ruler of a charity and its activities. For such people I have selected a song:

WHO ARE THE IMPOSTERS OF CHARITY

When the imposters of charity come to you, beware! Remember this song (written by another Morrison):

How can you stand the silence that pervades when we all cry?
How can you watch the violence that erupts before your eyes?
How can you tell us something just to keep us hanging on?
Something that just don't mean nothing, when we see it, you are gone.

Clinging to some other rainbow while we're standing, waiting in the cold.
Telling us the same old story, knowing time is growing old.

That was a wonderful remark
I had my eyes closed in the dark
I sighed a million sighs.
I told a million lies . . .
To myself . . . to myself

How can we listen to you, when we know your talk is cheap?
How can we ever question why we give more and you keep?
How can your empty laughter fill a room like ours with
joy?
When you're only playing with us like a child does with a
toy?
How can we feel the freedom or the flame lit by the spark?
How can we come out even, when our reality is stark?

That was a wonderful remark
I had my eyes closed in the dark
I sighed a million sighs.
I told a million lies . . .
To myself . . . to myself

—Van Morrison

WHO ARE THE IMPOSTERS OF CHARITY
MY TOP 10 LIST

1. **Class Action Trial Lawyers**
   Lawyers against the big tobacco firms class action suit
   in Florida won a giant settlement. The lawyers got paid
   first at $3.25 billion. The lawyers who worked on this

case made $200,000 an hour! It was yet to be determined who will receive the judgment awarded. The common man will see very few dollars from this landmark judgment. But if these attorneys made $200,000 per hour, they ought to give some back to charity.

2. **Any President of the United States**
   It's amazing that a Cabinet post has never been established for Secretary of Philanthropy! The President needs to work with charities at the highest level. This leadership could determine best who provides . . . the Government, or the charities.

3. **Any Masters of Business Administration School in our Nation**
   This includes Harvard University, Stanford University, University of Pennsylvania Warton School of Business, and others. These schools need to teach how business can donate and create funding pipelines for charities. Commerce could be designed without creating unrelated business taxable income and other restrictions. Yes, business is about making profits and it's also about providing for employees, their families and the community they live in.

4. **Charitable Phone Solicitors**
   These people are paid up to 50% of what they raise by representing a charity: Police Funds, Firemen Family Funds, Community Outreach Programs, and so on. The problem lies not in these causes, but whom they use to raise their funds. Everyone gets cheated in that deal—donor and charity.

5. **Most Politicians**
   They say a lot but don't really do anything that matters. When it comes to charity, you must stick with a single purpose and hold your resolve for the passion. If you want to help, you can't waiver. Politicians have to play each side of the fence to get re-elected. That's the nature of the beast.

6. **Financial Services Firms**
   All of you . . . where has the training been? Financial Planners take years to master charitable gifting techniques. Most stockbrokers never get around to being able to integrate these techniques into their businesses. Even the wealthiest clients have been neglected, and worse . . . misguided. It's time to get busy! Train your employees and get into the game!

7. **The English Language**
   New definitions in the dictionary are disguising what should be direct "straight talk" when it comes to the needy. Someone is not "vision impaired," he is blind. Let's just say it straight out! When it comes to seeing the problem, let's not hide it with politically correct language. It is of the utmost importance to stay away from "pasteurizing" the problem. It's time to stay away from politically correct and move to charitably correct.

8. **Cereal Boxes**
   Cereal boxes warn us, "The contents of this package may settle." When you open the box, it's about half full (or less). It's a crime, isn't it? All cereal boxes should be packed to the brim, otherwise we all feel a little cheated.

9. **The American Bar Association**
   This organization has not learned how to teach and spread the word regarding charitable planning. In 1999, 65% of all lawyers admitted to the bar didn't have a "drafted will" (a written will). The ability simply to draft documents doesn't mean you are a specialist and capable of complete advice when it comes to wealth preservation and charitable planning.

10. **Technology**
    Technology itself does not hold an ability to bring us together in a meaningful way. If we can conceive it, then we must achieve it. Technology is moving quickly, but charity is still in the slow lane. Bring on the "techies" so they can accomplish great things! As it stands today, technology has not brought community together. In fact, it may be a factor that continues to de-humanize us.

FALSE HOPE

As discussed in Chapter Two, nothing is worse than to over-promise and under-deliver. When I think of cruelty and hateful activity, what always comes to mind is "the lie" and how cruel a lie can be. There are many forms and degrees of lying, yet perhaps the cruelest lie of all is the half-truth, or, even worse, the false promise. The false promise leads to false hope. False hope is a greater tragedy than no hope at all. When the false hope is realized to be an absolute no-hope, then paralysis sets in. I've seen people sit down and become numb to everything once the false hope is proven false. The best way to avoid this is to ask yourself "What can I realistically accomplish, and do I have reliable sources?"

Anyone who consistently gives false hope will always be considered an imposter of charity.

Charity, as with many things, comes with responsibilities. Many times there is no second chance when it comes to meeting dire needs. Someone in real need can't afford to rely on a false promise. "I tried my best, but I just couldn't get the items to you." Not performing in charity can be extremely devastating, heart wrenching. No one keeps statistics on charities that are given resources and gifts yet may not perform with adequate resources. No regulatory agency actually checks into charities that are over-funded; no agency looks into charities that are under-funded. Just remember . . . do your best, be honest, and, last but not least, be realistic. It is not a violation to let a charity down. Anything you do will be appreciated. The most important guideline should be: "Do what you say you are going to do!"

Answers to Quiz:	Rating:
1) D	0–1 Wrong: A Robin Hood and a giver.
2) C or D	2 Wrong: Need Work
3) D	3 Wrong: You're not really getting it!
4) A	4+ Wrong: You are either an Imposter of Charity or charity doesn't show up on your radar screen!
5) B	
6) D	
7) D	

CONCLUSION

I f you had only one prayer left, what would you pray for? I would pray for the "end of charity." The end of charity means that everything we know and have experienced in our lives will always come out perfect from now on and until the end of time. The role you can personally play in making this happen is much greater than you think!

How do you get started?
What do you need to bring?
Don't try this at home!

How do you get started? You start by making a list of the goals you want to achieve. Some of those goals are financial goals and not social or charitable goals. It is admirable to give your fortune away to the needy, but there are limits. Leveraging your wealth could mean your giving actually grows due to prudent money management and tax management. Nothing in this book suggests you avoid paying taxes. However, this book does demonstrate tax management and utilizing legal trusts that can't be taxed as long as you are in the "giving game."

After you have made your list of goals, the next step is to set a time line for those goals. This will also require a schedule of the goals coming to fruition. The methods are time-tested, yet the monitoring of the goals becomes the hardest part. Things always pop up. There can be changes at work, changes at home, problems with kids . . . the list goes on and on.

What do you need to bring? You need to bring or gather all your financial information and all your family information: wills, trusts, inheritance, and so on. You should bring a list of ideas on how you would like to manage your giving. Also, bring your family and include them in the process, unless the children are very young. Philanthropy is a belief and a behavior. If your kids see you behaving in a philanthropic way, they will consider becoming philanthropic. However, there is no guarantee of this.

You should bring the research you've done on charities. You must do this research yourself. As a donor, you have the right to choose the needy causes. Charity is not what you have to do. It is what you want to do. Giving is still a personal thing. Make sure you bring any and all information you've read to educate yourself about having your own foundation. Family Foundations and the trend among organizations to allow donors more control over the use of your gift is now the trend. Should I use a private foundation? Should I use a support organization? Should I use a trust? Do I need to hire someone full-time to guide me in the area of my giving? If you are going to hire someone, then "trust" is the optimum word. You must really know someone you trust very well.

Don't try this at home. This is an understatement! The best way to design, implement and carry out your true desires, beliefs, goals and values is to conduct a search for a team. This team will be your "master planning team." This team will help you chart a course, which can turn your dreams for yourself, your family and others into a reality. This reality will exist in the most effective use of your financial capital and your social capital. This team must maintain a balance between the two. I've heard several very wealthy individuals say, "I'm going to give it all away." I've never seen anyone actually do that yet. This is because it is not realistic. Giving every cent away is not a wise goal. It is much better to build a financial model, which will provide for years to come. Remember, life is a marathon not a sprint. The charity also wants to stay in the race for a long time.

Who you choose to lead the team is important. That leader will not always be the CPA or the financial advisor, or the attorney, for that matter. As discussed in Chapter 7, pick your Robin Hood and make sure the "Merry Men" are merry!

The other reason you need a team is taxes. Taxes can wipe out your philanthropy if you're not careful.

THE TAX MAN COMETH

He Cometh When We Make Money!
Individual Income Tax   39.6% (highest rate)
Corporation Income Tax   38% (highest rate)
Alternative Minimum Tax (AMT)   28% (highest rate)
AMT is the minimum a taxpayer will pay regardless of how many deductions they take.

He Cometh When We Save Money!

Short term gains on your capital =	39.6%	(highest)
Long term gains on your capital =	20%	(highest)
Long term gains held more than		
5 years on capital =	18%	(highest)
Unrelated taxable business income =	varies	(highest)
Gift tax to children =	55%	(highest)

He Cometh When We Die!

Federal Estate & Gift Taxes =	55%	(highest)
Income tax rates imposed on IRAs,		
Pension Plans, ISAs, 401K Plans* =	39.6%	(highest)
Generation Skipping Tax (GST)		
Always taxes at: highest rate =	55%	(no reduction or scale)

- Estate Tax and Income Taxes can both be combined and assessed against these accounts.
- Heirs could pay up to 77% at the time of death!

Get your team together and let them devise the best strategy for you. They are professionals and will bring you astounding results.

THE FINAL WORD

Good philanthropy doesn't come overnight. The best ideas and the system for getting better ways to help charity into the mainstream is key. If our society is looking for a formula and wanting to crunch numbers above all else, that may be a mistake. Man's thinking and deductive reasoning may hold back our ability to help one another and also help the environment. More homeless shelters and soup kitchens are being built, but more endangered species are dying off at the same time. Where do we begin? Where do we stop? That question is bigger than most of us. That question is probably not one that we need to spend time pondering. Our hearts will tell us when to stop. Foundations and charities are trying to get smarter, but the trend is to show us what the charity has done, what it could it do with your money, and, if you give this money now, how long will it last?

Charities do need to become self-sufficient, and perhaps our brightest business minds can provide the road map. Business is about producing a structured organization that makes money. Why can't charities be structured to make money? We know that charities are not for profit, but nothing should keep them from being self-sufficient. The following quote from Dave Bristol should serve to describe the situation best: "There'll be two busses leaving the hotel for the ballpark tomorrow. The 2 p.m. bus will be for those who need a little extra work; the empty bus will leave at 5 p.m."

Improvement will be the true salvation of charities, which must put performance in the forefront. Let's all get started off in new directions, seeking new ways and ideas to facilitate more resources for our giving. Giving isn't really giving at all if we get satisfaction. This is where the transformation takes place. We ourselves feel good and get "filled up" about the gift we made. The social value of the gift is in the eye of the beholder. No one can accurately judge this except for himself. Financial wealth is important, but, in the long run, spiritual wealth will create the joyful memories we all cherish.

If someone you care for sits down beside you and cries on your shoulder, and that makes you feel good . . . then you're already on your way. If those tears are bothersome, then you have a long way to go, my friend.

Your actions are you! Be comfortable. Don't let others "rapid pace" things in your face with your giving. Remember, you're not giving because you *have* to. You're giving because you *want* to.

Do not fall prey to pride of ownership nor to the motives and accountabilities of the business world when it comes to charity. Remember, business is about your success or the success of your employees under a certain set of standards. In charity, everything works and nothing works. This is how you must understand it. You can't dot-com it, link it, hedge it, IPO-it, or reverse-merge it. Charity is about others . . . not about you.

Don't tell me how you're making a great living . . . show me how you are making a great life!

Close your eyes for a moment and see the smiles on the children's faces, or the tears in the mother's eyes when you have made contact, when you have made a difference. There is nothing like it. Don't be embarrassed to show your feelings when you know there is something bigger than you. There is no shame in dreaming or even being unrealistic. Leave behind profit and loss statements, the customers you have, the people you hire and promote. Caring will be the actual work product of charity. Don't let that escape you. How did Sir John Templeton achieve "reverse wealth"—giving away ten times to charity what he spends on himself each year? He understands the New Charity.

So, for all of you who desire wealth like Sir John Templeton, I say, "Never give up . . . just keep on giving!"

I'll end with the story of the old man and the young man. They were walking along the road and the old man said to the young man, "What do you care most about in life?"

The young man did not hesitate. He said, "I care about my success!" The young man then asked the old man, "Well, what is it that you care most about?"

The old man replied, "I'm old. I guess I only care about the success of other people now." He added, "I do have some advice for you, son. When something stands in your way or disappoints you, do not ask what this world is coming to. Rather, ask what is coming to the world."

You see, the old man knew something the young man didn't. Changing your life may not get you into Heaven or even get you a successful career, but changing the way you *look* at life is a good start.

I hope and trust that whatever the human race seeks to dream and achieve becomes reality. This book did not intend to ignore or diminish the struggle and the history of sacrifice that is so admirable throughout history. When it comes to charity, I further hope that we may all progress in the quest for sympathy and empathy. Empathy must evolve to "organized empathy." The equation has been solved and now is the time to put its effectiveness to work. The best is not only yet to come, the best will even get better! I urge all to seek the middle ground between the passion of giving and the guilt feelings that may be present when we realize that giving can also actually enrich us financially and with social recognition.

The new courtship between families, investors, business owners, professionals, and charities is just beginning. The old courtship of too little fundraising and not enough resources is fading away in favor of an energized spirit. The inspiration behind all this seems to be a perspective that the possibilities are endless. The view of the business world has gone past putting limits on anything; the sky is the limit. I believe the same will hold true for the charitable world as well. Therefore, I will be the first to ask the question. Will there ever be an end to all the endless possibilities we will see in the near future regarding our environment, social changes, human resources, health care, disease control and the pursuit of better life planning? Simply put, will there ever be an end to all the possibilities in charity itself? I fully expect to see these possibilities someday realized.

All of us must enjoy charity for what it is and what it has been for all of mankind. Charity is an investment in humanity. I truly believe that if we go with the premise that "charity is not an option," then we must commit to the most effective strategies that meet goals. It is not enough to just commit without a plan. Giving in simple terms begins the commitment, investing with a charity and strategic gifts increases the scope of the commitment. It also represents an investment none of us can afford to miss.

THE LIST OF MAYBE'S:

Maybe—We will cure cancer.

Maybe—We will stop domestic violence.

Maybe—We will win the war on drugs (the government has not come close).

Maybe—We will live with healthy family values and use families in the process instead of politicians.

Maybe—We can make school a safe place.

Maybe—Poverty and hunger can be abated forever.

Maybe—We can start replacing our precious forests and environment.

Maybe—We can keep thousands of animals from extinction.

Maybe—Common sense will rule the day and American's will see that we hold the power and the resources to make a difference. If we attempt to rely on any government, state or federal, we will be sorely disappointed.

MAYBE—these should not be viewed as maybe's. Ordinary people focused on making a difference can accomplish all these goals. Shame on us if we don't try to solve and provide resources for every need listed above.

This book was not written as a Christian book, nor is it a religious book. It was an important view of this author that a religious bias may keep certain people from reading this book. If Christians or any other religious faiths read this book, then that is a good thing and the intention of this author. Charities are "looking for a few good men," or, more accurately, "looking for millions of people who are committed to make a difference." All walks of life are included in this quest. I hope this passage in the Bible gives all of us a clear focus on what charity is and how the act of giving will change the outcome of human lives. This passage should not create any agenda toward Christianity and should not be viewed as serving that purpose. It is quoted because it was the most accurate account that this author has found regarding the act of giving, the rewards and the end result.

The Bible Speaks About Planned Giving

> One man gives freely, yet gains even more; another withholds unduly, but comes to poverty. A generous man will prosper; he who refreshes others will himself be refreshed.
> —Proverbs 11:24–25

This statement from the Bible represents a fact in today's world. It starts with the logic that anyone who gives freely will be enriched mentally, and the enrichment will also satisfy his or her soul. The phrase "become more wealthy" is more difficult to understand, and most people do not believe it because it defies logic. How could someone get wealth from giving away wealth? Believe it or not, some things in life defy logic! THIS IS ONE THING, I TELL YOU, THAT WILL DEFY LOGIC EVERY TIME! The word "charity" means something. It means work without expecting anything in return and the return will be greater than you expect.

Celebrity basketball game on behalf of Alliance Charity, the ***Robert Griffith Foundation.*** Kids pictured benefit from the Foundation in the form of scholarships.

NFL celebrity participants pictured: Jerome Bettis, Justin Armour, Shawn Springs, DeWayne Washington, Martin Bayless, Terrell Owens, Michael Pagan, Ryan McNeil.

Christmas "bikes" given out by Charitable Alliance to *Miracles in Motion Foundation* for poor and needy families.

ABOUT MITCHELL MORRISON

Mitchell Morrison has been involved in the insurance advisory and financial service industry since 1980. He is a charitable planning architect, helping clients and their advisors to clearly define problems, focus on objectives, and provide an abundance of solutions. After careful evaluation of all factors, he and his staff will implement "the road map" in meeting client goals. He is the president of Charitable Alliance Group located in Dana Point, CA.

In sharing his expertise with others, Mitchell has conducted over 2000 seminars on the topics of: Basic Investing, Risk Management, Retirement Planning, Advanced Stewardship, and Charitable Planning. Each year he continues to update his knowledge by attending numerous seminars and conferences on the latest tax, legal business planning, and issues to ensure his firm remains on the cutting edge. He is a Certified Estate Planner, member National Committee on Planned Giving, NIPA, IAFP, NASD series 7, 39, 63, and California Insurance Licensed. Mitch holds a B.A. in Journalism from the University of Southern California. He also attended George Washington University, Washington, D.C. where he obtained a Master of Science degree.

Mitchell has been involved with national and regional charities and industry memberships for numerous years. He is the current director of Worldwide Outreach for the World Bible Society and a past director of Doers Fellowship New Life Ministry, helping people living in Ukraine. He has traveled on missions throughout the United States and abroad and continues fund raising and public speaking on behalf of numerous charities, promoting his concept: "Would you give more to charity if charity allowed you more to give?"

Mitchell Morrison has been active in his community as a volunteer and attends Mariners Church in Newport Beach, California, where he resides with his wife, Bonnie, and their children, Reed and Kaylen. In his leisure, Mitch enjoys performing music, rollerblading, skiing, sporting events, boating, and fishing.

To order additional copies of

Have your credit card ready and call

Toll free: (877) 421-READ (7323)

or send $15.00** each plus $4.95 S&H* to

WinePress Publishing
PO Box 428
Enumclaw, WA 98022

www.winepresspub.com

**WA residents, add 8.4% sales tax

*add $1.00 S&H for each additional book ordered